Design

The *Fletchers* formed the largest class of destroyers ever built, and are regarded by many as one of the most successful. They served on active duty in the US Navy for thirty years and many survived in numerous other navies almost sixty years. It was not until 2001 that Mexico's *Cuitlahuac*, the former *John Rodgers* and the last active *Fletcher*, decommissioned.

To many these were the quintessential destroyers – the latest and most advanced flotilla craft of the period, they were roomy, well armed, able to absorb enormous punishment, and still capable of fighting. The *Fletchers* fought through most of the Pacific war, from the night battle of Guadalcanal (November 1942) onward, and their active careers spanned the Korean and Vietnam conflicts as well.

The *Radford* (DD 446) was one of the first *Fletchers* to complete and this photo taken on 7 August 1942, just after commissioning, shows the configuration of the earliest round-bridge ships. Note the tall two-level platform for the twin 40mm mount between Nos 3 and 4 gunhouses. (USN)

EVOLUTION OF THE DESIGN

Before the Second World War US destroyer design was influenced by two factors: Washington Treaty restrictions and the existing large fleet of obsolescent four-stack destroyers built for the First World War. Because of the large total tonnage of these four-stackers the treaty effectively restricted new US destroyer displacement to 1500 tons if enough were to be built. Also it constrained development in that no new destroyer designs were built until the launching of the *Farragut* class in 1934. This class set the standard for the pre-war destroyers: four or five 5in 38cal, eight to sixteen torpedo tubes, four depth charge throwers, two depth charge racks on the stern, and a scattering of light AA – at that time .50cal machine guns. These ships were overgunned for their displacement and by the time war broke out most had lost their fifth 5in gun.

The first classes of pre-war destroyers had the same hull. It was 341ft long overall with a beam of 35ft 6in. These ships also had a raised forecastle stepped down about 100ft from the bow. The next three classes – *Sims*, *Livermore* and *Gleaves* – were very similar in shape, but slightly longer and had a different bridge structure. These pre-war destroyers compared unfavourably in terms of size and armament with the destroyers of their likely adversaries, Germany and Japan. As war clouds gathered, the General Board of Naval Construction considered a destroyer free of treaty limitations that could be mass-produced for wartime purposes.

Interestingly, the initial requirement was for a lighter and faster version of the previous classes. The General Board was concerned about what they considered the excessive size of the *Benson* and *Gleaves* class destroyers, and wanted to return to the small fast torpedo boat role envisaged for US destroyers. The intention was for an inexpensive design that could be mass-produced for the oncoming war. The first step was to reduce weight by adopting a flush deck solution. Then the modifications came in: more ASW capability was required, so space had to be made for extra depth charge racks and throwers; more AA capability was wanted – so the aft deckhouse was stretched and a 1.1in quad (and some 20mm Oerlikons) added; for the Pacific high endurance was essential, requiring a few more fuel tanks here and there; enemy destroyers were quite large, so surface warfare capability required at least five 5in/38s; splinter protection was also increased. So there was a

The basic division in appearance between ships of the *Fletcher* class was the design of the bridge. The earliest ships had a rounded shape in plan view, but this was replaced by a more angular design with the bridge wings extended right round the front of the pilothouse. This layout was faster and cheaper to fabricate, but was also influenced to a degree by British experience which suggested the advantage to a CO of clear all-round vision during air attacks. This is *Burns* (DD 588), a square-bridge ship seen on 15 May 1943, shortly after commissioning. (USN)

certain inevitability that the small fast torpedo boat became the largest and slowest destroyer yet built by the US navy.

In any event this was a good thing. Although its nominal top speed was slightly less than the pre-war destroyers, in practice its more reliable machinery and hull form would enable it to go faster under combat conditions. The *Fletchers*, with their long thin hull, did suffer from a wide turning radius, but this was eventually fixed with a larger rudder.

The destroyer mission of the Second World War required a jack-of-all-trades. The *Fletchers*' even balance of surface weaponry, ASW capability, AA defence and protection made it the ideal destroyer for its time. It fought in numerous surface actions – in some cases taking battleships under fire. It screened fast carrier task forces, protecting the carriers from submarine attack and enemy aircraft. It also conducted the last US destroyer torpedo attacks at the battle of Leyte Gulf. The design was very successful. Indeed, they were so well regarded that the first post-war mass-production destroyer, the *Forrest Sherman*, began as a project for an updated *Fletcher*.

Below: A close-up of the round bridge of the *Radford* (DD 446), 20 November 1942. The electronics suite of these ships was very advanced for destroyers of their day. (USN)

Right: Another view of the *Radford* (DD 446) taken on 20 November 1942. Barely four months after commissioning modifications (ringed on the photo) have already been made. Compared with the earlier August view of the ship, the main visible difference is the lowering of the aft 40mm platform. (USN)

So this is what the General Board ended up with:

***Fletcher* Class Specification**

Dimensions		Length oa 376ft 6in, length wl 369ft, beam 39ft 8in, draft 22ft 8in
Height above water		Bow 19ft, stern 9ft, bridge 41ft, stack 47ft, mast 83ft
Displacement		2050 tons (standard), 2700 tons full load
Machinery		Two-shaft steam turbines, 4 B&W boilers, 60,000shp
Speed max (trial)		35.1kts @ 2800 tons
Endurance (trial)		4800 nm @ 15kts
Armament	**1942-43**	5 x 5in 38cal, 2 x 40mm, 6 x 20mm, 10 x 21in TT
	1943-45	5 x 5in 38cal, 10 x 40mm, 7 x 20mm, 10 x 21in TT
	1945	5 x 5in 38cal, 14 x 40mm, 12 x 20mm, 5 x 21in TT
Complement		9 officers, 264 men

With the *Fletcher* class the USN at last had a destroyer that was more than a match for German and Japanese destroyers. It was as large, fast, well armed and even more robust that its counterparts. The *Fletchers* were also much more sophisticated in terms of electronics and AA weaponry.

The key visible features that distinguished the *Fletchers* from the previous class were that they were flush-decked and 25 per cent larger. There were internal features that were ground breaking as well. The *Fletcher* introduced the CIC or combat information centre to destroyers. The days of the captain observing everything from the vantage point of the bridge were passed, and the ship's sensors now included radar, sonar, radio, sophisticated internal communication circuits to report damage and ship's status, as well as traditional visual signalling and lookout reports. The combat information centre served as a coordinating area for all of these sources of information. During battles information – often contradictory – came in thick and fast and the CIC served to sort, analyse and get a clear picture of the situation so that the captain could make informed decisions as to how to conduct the battle. As the war progressed the usefulness of the CIC became more and more recognised and by 1944 some destroyer captains were conducting battles from the CIC rather than the bridge. Initially the CIC was located in the bowels of the ship several decks below the bridge but as more captains used the CIC to direct operations it moved to the deckhouse just below the bridge.

Another important feature was the 'unit' system of propulsion. Essentially it was a duplicate power plant. There were two propeller shafts – each one was serviced by a separate fire room and engine room. This was so that no one hit would stop the ship. Even a lucky hit between the forward engine room and after fire room which disabled both would not stop the ship because the forward fire room could be coupled to the aft engine room, ensuring that propulsion was continued. This feature alone could be a battle winner – as evidenced by the *Fletcher* class destroyer *Johnston's* heroic fight against the Japanese main fleet even after severe damage to its engine rooms.

The size of the ships meant that, unlike many of the pre-war destroyers, they could take extra AA and ASW armament without affecting their fighting qualities and stability. As evidenced by the table above, AA armament increased from 4 x 20mm and 2 x 40mm to 12 x 20mm and 14 x 40mm – but not only were these weapons added but storage for the extra ammunition was needed, extra crew to man the weapons and extra space for the gun directors. Only the *Fletcher* class and its successors were capable of this level of expansion.

The electronics and fire control of the *Fletcher* class was very advanced for its time.

Fire control for the 5in guns was provided by a Mk 37 director above the bridge. Atop the director was a Mk 12 fire control radar and later in the war this was supplemented by the Mk 22 (or

A massive advantage of the *Fletcher* class was its relatively sophisticated fire control system. This is the Mk 37 main director, seen on the Mexican *Cuitlahuac* (ex-USS *John Rodgers*), the last of the class to remain in service. (Sea Photo - www.warship photos.com)

orange peel) operating in tandem. The 40mm twins and later quads were directed by the ubiquitous Mk 51 directors, although some of the early destroyers were commissioned with the Mk 49 version (early usage).

On the foremast the air search radar was the SC-2 with the IFF 'billboard' atop the radar added after 1943. Lower down the mast on a platform projecting forward was the SG radar used for surface detection. In 1942 SG was the most advanced radar afloat and the *Fletchers* were among the first ships to mount it. Had its capabilities been better understood by some of the admirals fighting night actions in the Solomon Islands, the outcome of several engagements might have been very different.

The rest of the electronic suite consisted of a range of radio communications circuits – VHF TBS (Talk-Between-Ships) antennas were quadrapoles mounted on the yardarm of the foremast; HF long distance communications used long antenna wires between the foremast and aft stack. Also on the foremast were sets of fighting lights – a set of three coloured lights which allowed the ship to identify herself in night battles. In addition, there were directional antennas to determine the bearing of enemy transmissions and on a few ships TDY jammers to try to jam those frequencies (often after determining the bearing).

For anti-submarine warfare the ships had a QC series 'searchlight' sonar dome, six depth charge throwers (K guns) located in the ship's waist abeam the aft deckhouse, and two racks on the stern. The *Fletchers* proved very effective submarine hunters.

The 5in 38cal was a proven weapon that was used in all of the pre-war destroyers. It was a dual-purpose gun that could be used against surface targets or aircraft. It had a rate of fire of over 15 rounds per minute and fired a shell weighing 54lb a distance of 20,000yds (although its accuracy limited it to an effective maximum range of 10,000yds). Later in the war a proximity fuse was introduced which enabled the shell to explode when it sensed that it was near an aircraft. For a 54lb shell 'near' was close enough to destroy the aircraft,

The 1.1in quad cannon in the original design was immediately supplanted by the 40mm AA gun. It was built under licence from a Swedish Bofors design. It had a maximum rate of fire of 100 rounds per minute and could fire a 2lb shell up to an altitude of 8000ft.

Below: The forward 5in guns of the *Kidd* (DD 661), seen on 7 August 1945. The US 5in 38cal was probably the best medium calibre dual-purpose naval gun of the war. (USN)

Bottom right: The 40mm was the US Navy's heaviest automatic AA gun. The *Fletcher* class were among the first ships armed with this weapon. By the end of the war some ships had as many as six twin mounts. This close-up of *Howorth* (DD 592) on 2 July 1945 shows the aft twin and its Mk 51 director. (USN)

The two quintuple torpedo tubes housed 21in torpedoes. These were inferior in range and warhead to the Japanese 'long lance' torpedoes, especially early in the war when they had defective guidance and fusing mechanisms. These were rectified by 1943 and despite being inferior to the 'long lance' it was still capable of inflicting enormous damage. Using only torpedoes *Fletcher* class destroyers sank a battleship in the Battle of Surigao Strait.

Six *Fletcher* class destroyers were redesigned to take a floatplane. They lost a 5in gun and a set of torpedo tubes so as to mount a cruiser-type catapult. There was no room for a hangar or a decent aircraft-handling crane – one was jury rigged on the port side. Only three saw service as such before the experiment was deemed a failure, and they were all rebuilt to the original design prior to entering the combat zone.

Above and below: Two close-ups of the 40mm twin at The National Museum of the Pacific War, Fredericksburg, Texas. (Sea Photo - www.warshipphotos.com)

The aft quintuple 2in torpedo tubes aboard the preserved *Kidd* at Baton Rouge, Louisiana. The 'doghouse' that used to protect the crew from the blast of No 3 gun has been removed, revealing the training apparatus. The *Fletchers* kept both sets of tubes until late in the war when the kamikaze threat saw many ships land their forward mount in favour of quad Bofors AA. (Sea Photo – www.warshipphotos.com)

POSTWAR

After the war the sheer numbers of *Fletchers* ensured a continued role well into the future. Although more modern designs took the front line duties away from *Fletcher* type destroyers, many were modernised and used as ASW and escort ships. The 21in quintuple mounts were replaced by anti-submarine torpedoes. The depth charge throwers were removed as well. The 40mm quads were replaced by the more effective 3in 50cal twins, and all of the by now ineffective 20mms were removed. In many the forward 5in mount was replaced by a large trainable hedgehog launcher; in others the mount was kept but the old 40mm positions had fixed hedgehog launchers.

Below: One of the floatplane conversions, the *Halford,* undergoing trials. The catapult is clearly visible on the aft deckhouse. (USN)

For a pre-war design the *Fletchers* proved remarkably capable of absorbing additional equipment and the resulting extra weight without too much degrading of their essential qualities. This is *Hazlewood* (DD 531) in September 1945, showing a typical war-end configuration, including the enhanced AA fit to counter kamikazes. (USN)

Careers

Since there were 175 members of this class it is impossible to chronicle the exploits of every ship, so what follows is representative. The *Fletchers* played a prominent part in the Second World War and afterwards so this section comprises a general history of the class, some notable battles that featured *Fletcher* class destroyers, and short histories of some of the more famous members of the class.

On 5 October 1942 the *Fletcher*, name ship of the 175 ships of its class, and *O'Bannon*, the second of this class, arrived in the South Pacific combat zone to form what became the Cactus striking force and later Destroyer Squadron Twenty-One (DesRon 21). Within a month they were in the thick of it, fighting in the wildest surface engagement of the war – the Battle of Guadalcanal on Friday the Thirteenth of November.

The Battle Of Guadalcanal

This confused action happened when a US task force of five cruisers and eight destroyers (amongst them was the *Fletcher* and *O'Bannon*) barged into the centre of a Japanese bombardment task force which included two battleships, a cruiser and no less than eleven destroyers. The Japanese were not anticipating any opposition and while the US force was expecting the Japanese, they were surprised to find themselves more or less in the centre of this force. The American Admiral, Daniel Callaghan, ordered his ships to open fire and his flagship, the *San Francisco*, promptly put several salvoes into the US cruiser *Atlanta*. Not to be outdone, the IJN battleship *Hiei* hit the destroyer *Yudachi* with its first salvo. When Admiral Callaghan realised that the *Atlanta* was his target, he ordered – perhaps accidentally – *all* of his ships to

The name ship of the class shortly after commissioning in mid-1942, demonstrating her less than ideal turning radius. (USN)

The *Radford* (DD 446) on 20 November 1942 before sailing for the South Pacific. The ship was to become a key member of Cactus Striking Force and earned a presidential Unit Citation for her activities in the Solomon Islands. (USN)

cease fire. This caused confusion in both the US and Japanese forces, but Callaghan was killed within a minute after this order (for the record by a Japanese salvo) and the situation then deteriorated into total chaos for both sides.

The *O'Bannon* was the fourth ship in the American column following three other destroyers of the lead division. These ships were the first hit by the enemy and the *O'Bannon* had to thread her way through sinking and damaged destroyers throwing liferafts and floatation material to survivors struggling in the water. One swimmer was sucked through the *O'Bannon*'s propellers but survived with minor injuries. Very quickly the *O'Bannon* was the lead ship of the column and took a nearby Japanese destroyer under fire and was scoring hits when Callaghan's message to cease fire came over the TBS circuit. By this time the *O'Bannon* was within 1800yds of the battleship *Hiei*. Ignoring Callaghan's last order, the *O'Bannon* closed to 1200yds of the *Hiei* for a torpedo attack – she was so close that the battleship's salvoes passed harmlessly overhead. The *O'Bannon* then fired three individually aimed torpedoes and had the satisfaction of seeing at least one explode. Unfortunately the detonators on the American torpedoes often exploded prematurely and this was the case on that night. She was coming on so close to the Japanese battleship that she had to reverse her engines to clear. The *O'Bannon* then checked fire and retired temporarily from the battle.

The *Fletcher* was the last ship in the column and was the last to get into the battle. By this time the situation was likened to 'minnows swimming in a bucket'. It was impossible to distinguish any semblance of formation of either side or recognise friend from foe. Using her modern SG radar the *Fletcher* was at least able to determine where ships were (but not which ones they were) and threaded her way through flaming wrecks and salvoes of all calibres seeking targets of opportunity. She spotted what appeared to be a Japanese heavy cruiser at 10,000yds and fired a salvo of torpedoes at her. All either missed or failed to detonate – a common failing of US torpedoes at this time of the war. In any event this was all to the good as the intended victim was probably the USS *Helena*.

This furious battle spluttered to an end about an hour after it erupted, with the majority of participants sunk, flaming wrecks or immobile. Those that could, withdrew. On the US side this was a small force of three destroyers: the undamaged *Fletcher*, the *O'Bannon* whose only battle injury was to her sonar equipment, and the badly damaged but still mobile *Sterrett*. They were accompanied by three cruisers – the heavily battered *San Francisco*, who had lost so many senior officers that she was under the command of the communication officer, Lt Cmdr McCandless; the *Juneau* whose keel was broken during the battle and had lost all radio communications; and the lightly damaged *Helena*. The two *Fletcher* class destroyers acquitted themselves well, fighting hard and escaping relatively unscathed. This was largely due to their superior radar and the inclusion of a combat information centre where all battle information was correlated and assessed.

The Battle of Tassafaronga

Within three weeks the *Fletcher* was in combat again, this time against a squadron of Japanese destroyers cruising off Point Tassafaronga in Guadalcanal. The *Fletcher* was the lead ship of a hastily assembled task group consisting of five cruisers and four destroyers. They surprised the Japanese, but there was confusion on the American side as well. The *Fletcher*, which had the unsuspecting Japanese force in radar contact and a torpedo solution in hand, did not get the go-ahead from the commanding Admiral, 'Bosco' Wright, until the Japanese force had already gone past. This required a following shot type of solution for the torpedo attack that was nowhere near as favourable as the initial position. The *Fletcher* fired her torpedoes and hauled clear as per her orders. The cruisers opened fire on the Japanese destroyers but were very inaccurate. Using the cruiser gun-flashes as a point of aim the Japanese launched their torpedoes (very accurately) and quickly turned away. Three US cruisers were severely damaged and a fourth, the *Northampton*, sunk at the cost of one Japanese destroyer sunk. The outnumbered Japanese destroyermen easily won this battle but the outcome might have been different if the *Fletcher* and her consorts had been allowed to launch a torpedo attack when they wanted to rather than wait for the Admiral's say-so. The *Fletcher* is remembered by the survivors of the cruiser *Northampton* as the one ship that returned to rescue survivors.

'Cactus Striking Force'

At about this time the *Radford* and *Nicholas* arrived in the South Pacific and the division of *Fletcher* class destroyers, now based at Port Purvis, adjacent to Ironbottom Sound, became known as the 'Cactus Striking force'. As such they participated in most of the surface engagements, shore bombardments, anti-submarine and air defence actions and amphibious landings throughout the Solomons chain.

Organised as a squadron in March 1943, there quickly developed an esprit de corps among officers and crews, knowing that they had been and were going to be the lead ships in surface engagements with the best of the Imperial Japanese Navy. In fact, to have the crews of ships in Tulagi harbour and Purvis Bay 'man the rails' to cheer DesRon 21 returning from a night action up the 'Slot' was pretty heady stuff.

In October 1943, the squadron was ordered north to the central Pacific to join the fast carrier task forces in the Gilbert and Marshall Islands campaigns. After that the squadron could be found supporting MacArthur's advance along the north coast of New Guinea and later it was to see action in most Pacific naval operations, ending with a leading role in the victorious entrance to Tokyo Bay for the Japanese surrender, in September 1945, before being disbanded.

LaVallette (DD 448) on 5 September 1942, another ship on her way to join DesRon 21, a mainstay of the destroyer war in the early years of the Pacific campaigns. (USN)

The *Jenkins* (DD 447) in Measure 13 Mod camouflage on 17 August 1942. The ship was painted Navy Blue on all vertical surfaces prior to arriving in the Solomon Islands to join DesRon 21. (USN)

Through these three years at war, the ships of DesRon 21 and its predecessor 'Cactus Striking Force' – *Fletcher* (DD 445), *Radford* (DD 446), *Jenkins* (DD 447), *LaVallette* (DD 448), *Nicholas* (DD 449, flagship), *O'Bannon* (DD 450), *Chevalier* (DD 451, sunk in surface battle, Solomon Islands), *Strong* (DD 467, sunk in surface battle, Solomon Islands), *Taylor* (DD 468), *De Haven* (DD 469, sunk by air attack in Ironbottom Sound, Solomon Islands) and replacements *Hopewell* (DD 681), *Howorth* (DD 592) and *Ross* (DD 563) – earned three individual Presidential Unit Citations and one Navy Unit Commendation in addition to 123 engagement stars on their collective Atlantic and Asiatic-Pacific Campaign ribbons,

Above: The *Charles Ausburne* (DD 570), the celebrated flagship of Arleigh Burke's DesRon 23 throughout the war (the ship was later transferred to the West German Navy). She appears here on 30 September 1944 after her first refit in a striking Ms 32/14D scheme. Also note the addition of Mk 51 gun directors and tubs atop the bridge. (USN)

Above right: Another view of the *Charles Ausburne* on 30 September 1944. The changes to the AA are clearly visible as is a small mast just forward of the 40mm tub. (USN)

DesRon 23 – the 'Little Beavers'

In September 1943 Desron 23 arrived in the Solomon Islands. Unlike the formation of Desron 21, where the destroyers were thrown into combat piecemeal upon arrival, Desron 23 had the luxury of training as a squadron. As such they were assigned all sorts of missions from screening amphibious landings, shore bombardment, barge-busting (shooting up convoys of troop-laden Japanese barges) and interception of enemy forces. They were kept so busy that the squadron's nickname was the 'Little Beavers'.

As a squadron they really proved their worth at the Battle of Empress Augusta Bay off the island of Bouganville in the northern Solomon Islands. The Americans had just landed a force of marines in Empress Augusta Bay, and the Japanese had counter-attacked the beachhead forces with a task force of two heavy and two light cruisers and four destroyers. To protect the beachhead was an American force of four modern light cruisers and the eight destroyers of DesRon 23. The squadron was commanded by Captain Arleigh Burke – who was later to become CNO - and his instructions to attack in divisions allowed a great degree of independence from the cruiser column. This was one of the first engagements where destroyers were allowed freedom to act independently, and they used it well.

The van division attacked first, unleashing 25 torpedoes at the head of the Japanese force. At the same time the Japanese force turned to close the American cruisers and out of the way of the torpedoes. Undeterred, the four van destroyers came in from the north later in the battle polishing off stragglers.

The rear division also attacked independently, firing torpedoes and taking targets under gunfire. By becoming so closely engaged with the enemy this force came under fire from both the US cruisers and the van destroyers. They torpedoed the light cruiser *Sendai* and sank the Japanese destroyer *Hatsukaze* and chased the stragglers back towards Rabaul before rejoining the cruiser force just before dawn.

The Battle of Cape St George – Destroyer versus Destroyer

On 25 November 1943 South Pacific headquarters got wind of a Japanese destroyer mission just north of Bougainville. DesRon 23 was the only force available to disrupt the Japanese so Halsey enquired of Arleigh Burke what speed his destroyers could make. Burke replied '31 knots'. To this Halsey sent the famous order:

> 31 Knot Burke – get this. Put your squadron athwart the Buka-Rabaul evacuation line about 35 miles west of Buka. If no enemy contacts by early morning come south to refuel same place. If enemy contacted you know what to do. Halsey.

At one in the morning the Japanese force – consisting of destroyers *Onami*,

Makinami, *Amigiri*, *Yuguri* and *Uzuki* – appeared on the radar screens of three of Burke's destroyers. Burke gave chase to the unsuspecting Japanese (they had no radar) using the time-honoured tactic of having one division attack while the other provided cover. The three lead destroyers unloosed 15 torpedoes at the Japanese and sank the *Onami* and disabled the *Makinami*. The other three Japanese destroyers scattered but Burke kept his division of three destroyers concentrated and directed the other division to finish off the *Makinami*. Choosing the largest target of the three remaining destroyers, the *Yuguri*, Burke sped after them. A stern chase is a long chase but '31 Knot Burke' wasn't to be deterred. Pouring on nearly 35 knots and swerving to avoid enemy torpedoes he managed to get within gunfire range of the *Yuguri*. Using the forward 5in mounts his ships were able to disable and then sink the hapless *Yuguri*, but the other two were too far ahead to catch and got away. Three Japanese destroyers were sunk without a single casualty to the destroyermen of DesRon 23.

After this battle there was a long hiatus of surface contact between Japanese and Allied forces. The ever more numerous *Fletcher*s busied themselves with screening carrier forces, supporting amphibious landings, submarine hunting and all of the various tasks that befell destroyer forces. However, the *Fletcher*'s biggest wartime moment was yet before them.

Leyte Gulf

The zenith of the *Fletcher*s' wartime career was the largest naval battle in history where a handful of *Fletcher* class destroyers determined the course of the battle.

What is called the Battle of Leyte Gulf actually consisted of four separate major engagements and *Fletcher* class destroyers had a leading role in two of them. For this battle the Japanese had three principal forces. One, consisting of four aircraft carriers (with minimal aircraft embarked), was to lurk off the north cape of the Philippines (Cape Engano) and decoy the powerful US Third Fleet away from protecting the transports in Leyte Gulf. The other two forces were to perform a pincer movement and destroy the relatively unprotected transports in the gulf. The southern pincer, made up of two battleships, four cruisers and eight destroyers, broken into two different forces, approached via Surigao Strait; the more powerful northern force comprised five battleships (including the *Yamato* and *Musashi*, the largest battleships ever built), twelve cruisers and twelve destroyers. In the course of the battle both these pincers were blunted by small groups of *Fletcher* class destroyers.

Surigao Strait

The southern force, consisting of the battleships *Fuso* and *Yamashiro*, heavy cruiser *Mogami*, and four destroyers, managed to avoid most of the air strikes of the powerful US Third Fleet and on the night of 24-25 October approached the Allied landing force in Leyte Gulf via Surigao Strait.

The Allies knew they were coming and at the head of the strait Admiral Oldendorf waited with a fully prepared force of six battleships and eight cruisers. Screening them were elements of Destroyer Squadron 24 (all *Fletcher* class DDs) under the command of Captain McManes. The Japanese southern force did not really have a chance, but just to make absolutely sure of things the commander of Destroyer Squadron 54, the inappropriately named Captain Coward, submitted a proposal to Admiral Oldendorf that elements of his destroyer squadron go further down the strait to deliver a torpedo attack on the approaching force. Oldendorf approved the plan immediately.

Melvin (DD 680), seen here on 30 September 1943, was nicknamed the Blue Devil for the Navy Blue Measure 21 camouflage she wore throughout the war. This destroyer is credited with sinking the battleship *Fuso* with one torpedo spread during DesRon 54's attack in the Surigao Strait (25 October 1944). (USN)

So at 02:30 on 25 October five *Fletcher* class destroyers (the *Melvin*, *McGowan* and *Remey* on the eastern side of the straight and *McNair* and *Monssen* on the western side) were heading south to deliver a surprise torpedo attack on the approaching Japanese force. The air was hot and

Killen (DD 593) on 8 June 1944. A few months later as a member of DesRon 24, whe was in action in the Surigao Strait against a powerful Japanese surface force that was largely destroyed by the torpedo attacks of *Fletcher* class destroyers. (USN)

humid that night and the sea as calm as glass. There was lightning on the hills bounding the strait. At 02:40 the *McNair* picked up the enemy column, on radar. Four Japanese destroyers were leading the column followed by the flagship *Yamashiro*, then the *Fuso* and the *Mogami*. The two forces were closing at a combined rate of 45kts. At 03:00 the destroyers of Captain Coward's squadron started launching torpedoes at the approaching Japanese. Within nine minutes 47 torpedoes were in the water heading for the Japanese force. It was a classic 'anvil' attack, torpedoes coming in from both sides off the bows. If the Japanese turned to comb the torpedoes coming from the port bow they exposed their broadside to the torpedoes coming into the starboard bow. The normally sharp-eyed lookouts in the Japanese ships did not spot Coward's destroyers until it was too late, and the torpedoes sank the battleship *Fuso* and a destroyer, as well as disabling two more destroyers. They also scored a hit on the other battleship, the *Yamashiro*, but it did not disable her. Captain Coward's destroyers then quickly retired, barely seen by the enemy and untouched by enemy fire.

Next in line for attack were Captain McManes's six destroyers, the Australian *Arunta*, and *Fletcher* class *Hutchins*, *Bache*, *Daly*, *Beale* and *Killen*. They attacked the depleted Japanese, who were ready by now for action. These destroyers succeeded in hitting the flagship *Yamashiro* one more time and polishing off one of the destroyers crippled by Captain Coward's squadron. By this time only three ships of the Japanese – the wounded battleship *Yamashiro*, the heavy cruiser *Mogami* and the destroyer *Shigure* – were left to face the waiting allied battle line. The overwhelming firepower quickly destroyed the *Yamashiro*, heavily damaged the *Mogami* (which sank a few hours later), only the lucky *Shigure* surviving. The southern force was utterly destroyed, the majority of it by a handful of *Fletcher* class destroyers. They were skilfully handled in what was to be the last fleet action where battleship gunfire and classic destroyer torpedo tactics were employed.

Off Samar Island

The Japanese northern force had been attacked by Halsey's Third Fleet on the 24th, with its massive airpower conducting no fewer than 1000 sorties. They sank the giant battleship *Musashi* and severely damaged the heavy cruiser *Myoko*. This force was observed to turn away from its objective after the *Musashi* sank. The Third Fleet then turned its attention to the decoy force of Japanese aircraft carriers to the north of it. Admiral Kurita, commander of the northern force, decided to reverse course again, heading his still formidable force of four battleships, eight cruisers and ten destroyers towards the Allied amphibious force in Leyte Gulf via the now unguarded San Bernadino Strait. They came through in the early hours of the morning and had steamed unobserved for six hours down the coast of Samar Island until at 06:45 they came into contact with Task Group 77.1.2 (known as Taffy 3 after its call sign).

The *Hoel* (DD 533) as she appeared on 25 October 1943. The *Hoel* led the torpedo attack of the screen destroyers against the entire Japanese northern force off Samar Island exactly a year later. She was sunk for her efforts. (USN)

Taffy 3 was a support unit, not intended for frontline combat with surface ships. It consisted of six escort carriers (slow vulnerable ships intended for convoy protection and amphibious landing support), four destroyer escorts and three *Fletcher* class destroyers: the *Johnston*, *Heermann* and *Hoel*. At 06:45 this force was oblivious of any threat, assuming that Halsey's Third Fleet was protecting them from the northern force. Three things happening in quick succession made the commander of Taffy 3, Admiral Clifton Sprague, aware of his dire predicament. His radio operators reported hearing Japanese 'gabble' at close range; within a minute one of the pilots operating off the escort carriers reported strange ships with pagoda masts just north of the force; and a few minutes later the powerful northern force appeared over the horizon and commenced fire.

The destroyer *Johnston* was closest to the Japanese. She was commanded by commander Ernest E Evans, an aggressive Cherokee. When he took command a year before, he announced to his crew that he wanted to take his ship in harm's way. So far he had had no contact with the Japanese fleet but when the pagoda masts appeared on the horizon he knew that this was just what he had been waiting for. Without stopping for orders, he steered the *Johnston* towards the Japanese northern force, laying smoke to screen the carriers and firing at the nearest Japanese ship, the heavy cruiser *Kumano*. Surrounded by shell-splashes from cruisers, battleships and destroyers the *Johnston* kept attacking, firing over 200 rounds and observing numerous hits. Closing to within 10,000yds she fired her ten torpedoes at the heavy cruiser and one of them hit and blew her bow off. The *Kumano* was out of the fight and the *Johnston* was as yet untouched. This changed three minutes later when the *Johnston* was hit by three 14in shells from a battleship and three more 6in shells from a light cruiser. Lt Hagan, the *Johnston*'s gunnery officer, reported: 'these hits knocked out the after fire room and engine room, lost all power to the steering engine, all power to the

A rare view of the short-lived *Johnston* (DD557). Known as 'GQ Johnny' because she was always courting action, the ship is one of the best-known *Fletchers*. She won a Presidential Unit Citation for single-handedly foiling the torpedo attack of a Japanese destroyer squadron during the Battle of Leyte Gulf. (USN)

after three 5in guns and rendered the gyro compass useless.' In addition, the radar was destroyed but the guns were still working, the steering and the aft three mounts could be operated manually and the *Johnston* could still make 17kts. The *Johnston*'s war was not finished yet.

Just after the *Johnston* turned to attack the Japanese fleet, Admiral Sprague ordered the screening destroyers to make a torpedo attack. The *Hoel* was near the *Johnston* and followed her in towards the Japanese fleet. She made smoke to screen the carriers (which had sought temporary refuge in a rainsquall) and opened fire on the battleship *Kongo*. The *Hoel* scored numerous 5in hits but did not do much damage to the well protected *Kongo*. She then fired a half salvo of torpedoes at the *Kongo*, but all missed. In turn the *Hoel* was hit in her after fire room and lost three guns as well from enemy heavy calibre fire.

The *Heermann* was on the disengaged side of the task force and was not able to get into position for the first attack, but after an hour of combat and evasive tactics, Sprague ordered another torpedo attack by the destroyers, this time accompanied by the destroyer escorts. The *Heermann* had a full load of torpedoes, the injured *Hoel* had fired half of hers, and the *Johnston* (also damaged) had none left. Nevertheless, when Commander Evans saw the other ships going in for a torpedo attack he joined in, to provide support and confuse the enemy.

As the makeshift attack unfolded, the *Heermann* led the two other destroyers and four DEs towards the Japanese force. The *Heermann* fired 7 torpedoes at the heavy cruiser *Haguro* and fired at the battleship *Kongo* with her 5in guns as well. After launching her last three torpedoes at the *Kongo*, the *Heermann* then retired, making smoke to screen the escort carriers. She was undamaged. The *Hoel* fired at the *Haguro* and the cruiser returned the compliment. The *Hoel* then aimed her remaining torpedoes at the *Haguro*, but they missed and instead ran straight at the flagship *Yamato*. The *Yamato* turned away from the oncoming torpedoes and removed herself from the battle for the next half hour. Unfortunately, the *Hoel* was permanently removed from the battle shortly after her heroic attack. She was hit over forty times by 5in, 8in, 14in and 16in shells. No destroyer could stand up to that kind of punishment and at 08:35 she was abandoned and the ship sank shortly afterwards.

The damaged and torpedo-less *Johnston* came in for the second attack, firing her main battery at all targets of opportunity, which included the battleships *Kongo* and *Haruna* and any number of heavy cruisers. At this time Admiral Kurita ordered a destroyer attack of his own. Four Japanese destroyers lead by the light cruiser *Yahagi* steamed towards the escort carriers of Taffy 3. The *Johnston* was in a position to interdict and she did. The *Johnston* placed herself directly in the path of the oncoming destroyer force, scored some hits on the *Yahagi* and forced the destroyers to fire their torpedoes prematurely. But *Johnston*'s number was up – after the Japanese destroyers fired their torpedoes they turned their attention to the solitary and disabled *Johnston*. An avalanche of shells destroyed her remaining fire room, communications were lost throughout the ship and only one gun was able to function. At 09:45 the *Johnston* was abandoned. The Japanese destroyers closed in and destroyed the abandoned hulk. The captain of one of the Japanese destroyers was said to have saluted as the *Johnston* rolled over and sank.

While the destroyers were protecting the escort carriers, the Japanese force was attacked by all the aircraft that could be launched by Taffy 3's escort carriers. Taffy 2 and Taffy 1 sent what they could as well. So bewildered was Kurita by the ferocity of an onslaught by what turned out to be a vastly inferior force that he felt that there must be something larger lurking over the horizon. His formation was a mess, thanks in large part to the repeated attacks by the American destroyers, so at 09:30 Kurita retired from the scene of the battle.

In both battles described above, the *Fletcher* class were able to display their offensive and defensive qualities: in Surigao Strait their CIC and superior radar enabled them to attack undetected; off Samar their compartmentalisation – particularly having staggered engine rooms and fire rooms – enabled them to sustain severe damage and still remain in combat. Of course the bravery with which the men aboard fought these magnificent ships was the most important factor.

After Leyte Gulf the Japanese Navy was more or less finished as a serious threat, but the war was by no means over for the *Fletchers*. Almost all the class were in the Pacific, screening the fast carrier forces, supporting

The *Kidd* (DD 661) in February 1945. The *Kidd* was seriously damaged by kamikazes late in the war, but she was repaired and kept as a museum ship and can now be seen at Baton Rouge, Louisiana. (USN)

amphibious landings and escorting service squadrons. Their role as attack units was diminished, although several *Fletchers* were involved in the last surface engagement of World War Two (a small skirmish with Japanese destroyers in the Philippines).

As they approached Japan the fighting got fiercer, and in terms of combat and casualties their biggest battle was yet to come. The era of the kamikaze had arrived. When Luzon was invaded the amphibious force was subjected to severe suicide attacks, which were fought off by the screening destroyers, many of them *Fletcher* class.

Okinawa

After the landings on Okinawa, the Japanese attacked furiously with kamikaze planes. The destroyer forces – by now predominantly *Fletcher* class – suffered their worst losses of the war. They had to stay on station for weeks and were attacked on a daily basis. Ten *Fletcher* class destroyers were sunk and as many more severely damaged at Okinawa. The story of the *Cassin Young* is an example of the sort of travails endured off Okinawa.

The *Cassin Young* took station as a radar picket (used for early detection of swarms of kamikaze) 30 miles north of Okinawa on 12 April 1945. At 13:37 three Val dive-bombers were sighted and the *Cassin Young* opened fire. She sent one plane down in flames but the lead plane, after diving at the ship, pulled out and crashed fifteen feet off her port quarter. Six more Vals came in for attack: five were splashed – one uncomfortably close – and the sixth came in strafing, hit the foremast and its bomb exploded just above the ship, blasting the decks with shrapnel and wounding 58 and killing one. The *Cassin Young* needed a month to repair the battle damage before she was on picket duty again. On 29 July, less than three weeks before the war ended, she was on station as a radar picket. At 02:11 radar contact was made on a very slow plane 20 miles away, so the destroyer went to flank speed and took the contact under radar-controlled fire. The target was reported to have gone down, but at that time a plane – possibly a second one – crashed into the ship at main deck level, destroying all radio and radar equipment and rendering the forward fire room unusable. Sixteen men were killed outright, including the captain, and the *Cassin Young*'s war was over.

Post-war

After the Second World War *Fletcher* class destroyers served in the US Navy in Korea and some even in Vietnam. Thirty-two were transferred to the navies of Argentina, Brazil, Chile, Columbia, Germany, Greece, Italy, Japan, Korea, Mexico, Peru, Spain, Taiwan and Turkey. By 1971, all ships remaining in the US Navy had decommissioned. The survivors served longer in the various foreign navies, and it was not until 2002 that the last active *Fletcher* decommissioned: Mexico's *Cuitlahuac*, the former *John Rodgers*.

The last serving *Fletcher* was the Mexican Navy's *Cuitlahuac* (ex-*John Rodgers*, DD 574). As shown here, the ship was little modified from her 1945 appearance, and as both the last round-bridge example and the most highly decorated of the surviving *Fletchers*, she was an obvious candidate for preservation. It is planned to turn the ship into a museum at Mobile, Alabama. (Sea Photo - www.warshipphotos.com)

Model Products

Skywave: Callaghan, 1/700 scale

For years this was the mainstay of 1/700 *Fletcher* kits. It was an advance on the Skywave S500 series kit and, as W1, it was the first kit in their well-known W series of Second World War ships. This kit was well regarded in its time but now the detail seems a bit clunky.

This kit can be built as a square- or round-bridge *Fletcher* – parts are included for both. There is also a sprue to build it as a post-war FRAM conversion but the moulded-on deckhouse is very definitely for a mid-war AA fit, so some difficult surgery will be required. The box art by Y Yoshida is lurid and exciting and shows the *Callaghan* in Measure 33 D camouflage steaming at high speed in company with another *Fletcher* DD. Although it is not as detailed as other box art, it is a useful reference for a mid-war *Callaghan*.

As to the specifics of the kit, the hull comes with the midships deckhouse integral, along with the side depth charge racks and nice thin midships splinter shields, although there are no limber holes under them. The side depth charge racks are just rectangular blobs of plastic and should be replaced by aftermarket parts.

Although the hull measures out correctly as to length and beam, it looks boxy and does not quite seem to replicate the graceful sheer of the *Fletchers*. The deckhouses are devoid of detail such as ladders, doors, piping, etc, so for extra detailing the modeller will have to resort to photo-etch. To the habitual 'superdetailer' this can be a blessing in disguise as the moulded-on details can be sanded off and replaced with the more precise and sharp edged photo-etch, brass wire and strip styrene.

The weapons are mostly over-scale and clunky, particularly the 40mm and 20mm. The same applies to the Mk 51 40mm directors – a rectangular prism on a pedestal. The 5in gunhouses are to scale but lacking hatches, ladders and other detail; the gun barrels are too thick and the blast bags are way over scale. Torpedo tubes are well detailed but the forward set does not have the training equipment atop them. The 26ft whaleboats are nicely done but not a good replica of the actual whaleboat; the seats are incorrectly placed and there is no engine in the middle. The stacks are not quite the right shape and thickness but the forward stack, alone amongst all the 1/700 *Fletcher* models has the sirens and platform. The instructions are easy to follow and written in Japanese and English (sort of). There are some useful camouflage patterns for Ms 12 Mod, Ms 31 D, Ms 32 D and Ms 33 D.

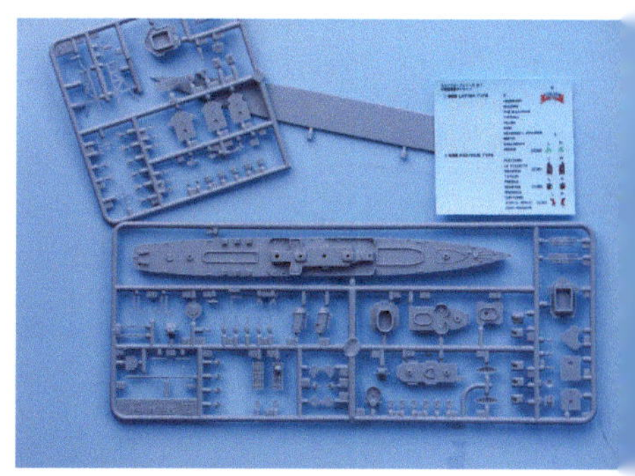

In summary this kit is fairly good and can be made much better by substituting aftermarket parts – ironically manufactured by the same company that produced this model – and adding photo-etch. The principal failing is that it does not quite catch the grace and sheer line of the *Fletchers* and this is very difficult to correct.

Tamiya: *Fletchers*, 1/700 scale

This kit appeared in the mid 1990s as an alternative to the Skywave kit. It represents the *Fletcher* as launched in 1942. There are enough parts included that would indicate that it could be built as a round-bridge *Fletcher* with a mid-war armament but the deckhouse is only set up for the early-war configuration.

The box art is more accomplished than Mr Yoshida's on the *Callaghan* but not as exciting. It represents the *Fletcher* as she was fitting out prior to entering the combat zone in October 1942. It does serve as a very useful reference for superdetailing the kit. There is good representation of a number of items such as ship's siren, fighting lights, rigging spreaders, railing and other items not included in the kit to help with superdetailing.

As is the case for other Tamiya kits it is well proportioned and fits together well. The hull shape in particular is an improvement over the Skywave offering, and better represents the graceful sheer and beautiful lines of these ships. The midships deckhouse is on the hull as are the side and rear depth charge racks. The side depth charge racks are not well done – they look like a rectangular prism and will look awkward next to the rather lovely K-gun part next to them. The rear depth charge racks are better but are in the wrong place. This ship can be built out of the box to represent the first seven *Fletchers* to be commissioned. This is because the aft deckhouse between gunhouses 3 and 4 is raised. This was done only for the earliest ships in the class, which were initially fitted with 1.1in quads atop this deckhouse. All the other round-bridge *Fletchers* had this deckhouse lowered 5ft with twin 40mm and the director at the same level. There is a part for this gun tub included in the kit but the deckhouse should be modified to fit it.

There are two flying bridge parts – early-war and late-war (with platforms for Mk 51 AA directors) but this is unusable on this kit as there is no place to put the 40mm twins on the deck below – the gun tubs are for 20mm only and it would require some major surgery to enlarge them. The kit includes five 40mm twins but in this kit there is no place to put four of them. These parts are strange: they are over-scale and do not look at all like a twin 40mm mount.

As to the other parts, the whaleboats are a good shape and contain the correct arrangement of seats, etc; the 5in gunhouses are too small and have very little detail. The 20mms are OK and closer to scale than the other 1/700 kits. The stacks are nicely proportioned and are an improvement on the chunky ones provided with the Skywave kit.

This Tamiya kit is intriguing in that it has no surface detail such as doors, hatches, portholes, ladders and piping on the superstructure. This provides for a rather plain out-of-the-box build but modellers who like to superdetail their kits will find this a bonus. Many superdetailers have to sand off plastic surface detail and replace it with photo-etch doors, ladders hatches etc. Since the basic shapes and fit of this kit is very good, superdetailers will be pleased with this kit. The instructions have a history of the *Fletcher* and its class in Japanese and a sort of English. On the back of the box there is a camouflage diagram of the starboard side of the *Fletcher* in Measure 12 Mod dapple pattern which she wore after commissioning and prior to her entry into the combat zone in October 1942.

Overall this is a good but not great kit. The basic shapes are right and the bulwarks and splinter shields are fine but detail is lacking and some of the small parts are poor.

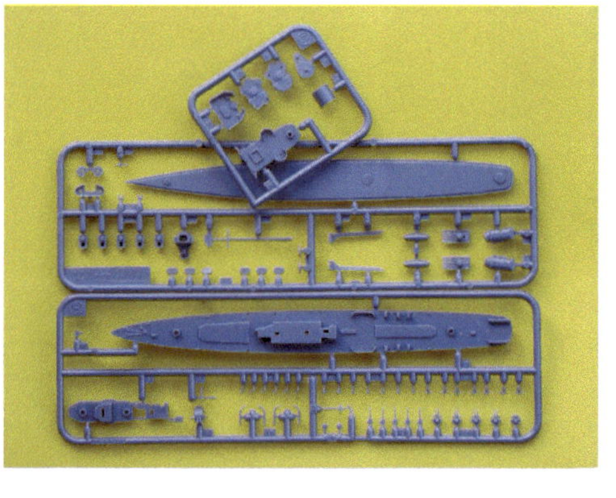

Tamiya: *Cushing*, 1/700 scale

The Tamiya *Cushing* is almost the same kit as the *Fletcher* but with a different casting for the hull/deckhouse and parts included for a square-bridge *Fletcher* with mid-war armament. The box art is nicely executed and will make an excellent reference for building the *Cushing* as she appeared in 1944.

The hull piece has a midships deckhouse with platforms for twin 40mm abreast the aft stack. The forward deckhouse has enlarged gun tubs so that 40mm twins can be placed there as well.

The mid-war components, such as the flying bridge with platforms for Mk 51 directors included in the *Fletcher* kit previously described, can be used with this kit to make a mid-war round-bridge *Fletcher*.

The instructions provide a diagram of the port side Ms 31 16D camouflage that the ship was painted in 1944. The starboard side is shown on the back of the box.

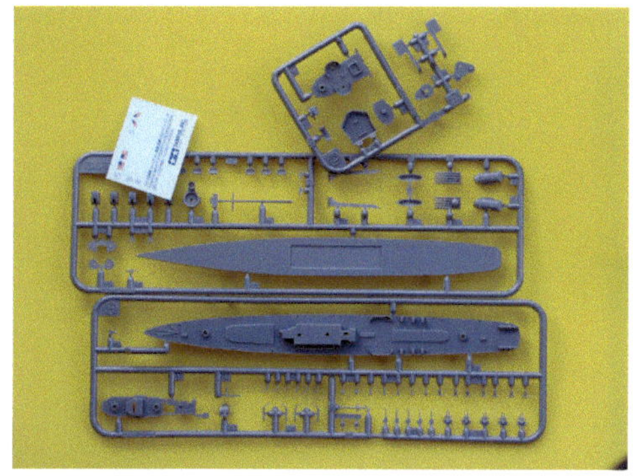

Trumpeter: *The Sullivans*, 1/700 scale

The Sullivans by Trumpeter is the best of the 1/700 *Fletcher* kits on the market at present. It represents a square-bridge *Fletcher* in a late-war configuration and can be built waterline or as a full-hull model. The box art is clunky and amateurish – it is correct in appearance but, with the exception of the rigging, which is well done, it is too featureless to be of much use for superdetailing. Remember the exciting paintings by John Steel on the Revell kits?

The hull and deck are separate parts in this kit. The hull shape appears satisfactory and captures the lines of a *Fletcher* well. It is also well down in the water, reflecting the deep draft of the overweight late-war destroyers. The surface detail on the decks is limited to hatches, hawse holes, anchor chain, capstan and bollards. Items such as deckhouses, depth charge racks, splinter shields, bulwarks that are on the other kits in this scale are separate parts. These parts are very well done – especially the side and aft depth charge racks. The bulwark that comes up from the hull protecting the middle deckhouse is well done with fine limber holes along the bottom.

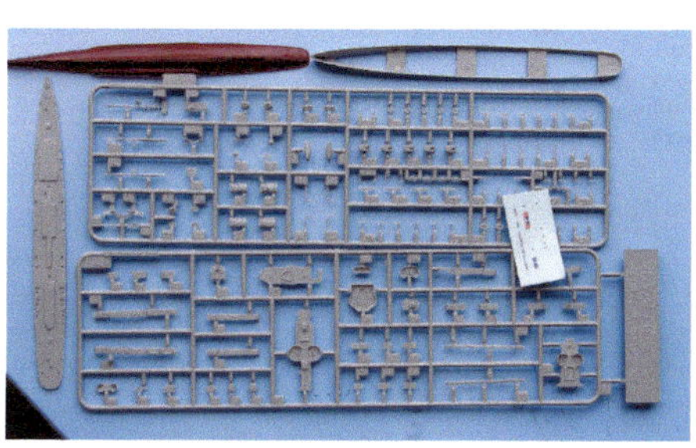

The deckhouses have a good amount of surface detail with the hatches and doors in the correct places. The detail is a little heavy however, and some modellers may wish to replace it with photo-etch parts.

The 5in guns are very nice. The front face of the gunhouse has the railings and hatches moulded on. They also have two other subtle details missing from all other kits in this area: the mount appears slightly off centre – which is correct, the gun is on the centreline but there is more space on the right of the gun. Also gunhouses on the main deck are slightly different from the ones above them. They have an extra knuckle on the roof that is barely perceptible both in the kit and in photographs of the real thing – but it's there.

The 36in searchlights are lovely – the searchlight rests in the cradle just lightly attached – not just a blob of plastic with the pedestal, cradle and searchlight as one solid piece. Other nicely done parts are the K-guns for the depth charges and the side depth charge racks. The 40mm quads are a set of two twins – just like the real thing. They are the correct size, and look as good as can be achieved with injection moulding technology, but the barrels have no taper and are too thick. The mast has a fair bit of detail including recognition lights and a decent taper but the detail is heavy and the SK-2 radar is too low and thick.

The instructions are very impressive. They have detailed assembly drawings as well as a colour section showing the various paint schemes. This section also has excellent detail and other items that will be very useful to superdetail the kit.

However, there are some flaws. The whaleboats are poor, the wrong shape and incorrect inside. The stacks have very nice detail – including an open grille on the cap and a very good representation of the piping aft of each stack – but the basic shape is not quite correct. It is a bit slab-sided whereas the actual stack is more rounded. The 20mm should be twins for this configuration – instead they are a very poor representation of a single.

In summary this is a very good kit and the only one in this scale in plastic that represents a late-war *Fletcher.* Although there are a few weak spots they are more than outweighed by the good parts – especially the 5in gunhouses and searchlights.

Other kits in this scale these are generally resin kits and out of production plastic kits.

Samek Models:
The Sullivans, 1/700 scale

This is a resin kit from the Czech Republic of *The Sullivans* in a late-war configuration. Although not generally found in hobby stores it is still in production and can be ordered online or from various mail order hobby outlets. This is a very nice kit but pretty much superseded by the Trumpeter kit. It does have some photo-etch included and has proper twin 20mm cannons.

Matchbox/AMT/Hawk:
Fletcher, 1/700 scale

This kit has been around for over thirty years and is pretty basic. The plastic comes in two colours – one a sort of Haze Gray and the other Navy Blue so that it can be assembled in a Ms 22 scheme (not really). The splinter shields are very thick and the light armament is grotesque. However the basic shape is correct and other than the Trumpeter kit it is the only one to have the correct shape of the gunhouses.

Bureau of Small Warships:
Fletcher, 1/700 scale

This is a resin kit from Los Angeles of the *Fletcher* in an early-war configuration. This kit is out of production and the Bureau of Small Warships has stopped trading. This is a very nice kit but pretty much superseded by the Tamiya kit, although the thinness of splinter shields and level of detail is better than the Tamiya kit.

Skywave:
Fletcher, 1/700 scale

This kit is a predecessor to the *Callaghan* kit. It comes two in a box and as a round-bridge *Fletcher.* The moulding is similar but not identical to the *Callaghan* and the comments about the *Callaghan* apply here – even more so.

Tamiya: *Fletcher*, 1/350 scale

This is the best *Fletcher* kit on the market. It is well researched, has a great amount of lovely detail, fits together beautifully and is very nicely moulded with no flash or sink holes.

It represents the *Fletcher* as first commissioned. There are virtually no extra parts to make it as anything else than the *Fletcher*, *Radford*, *Nicholas*, *Jenkins* or *O'Bannon* in 1942. They had a raised deckhouse between gunhouses 3 and 4 and the kit depicts this. It also has a part for the top of the lowered deckhouse with the 40mm twin and director in the same tub but no deckhouse to fit underneath it, nor does this part appear anywhere in the instruction sheet.

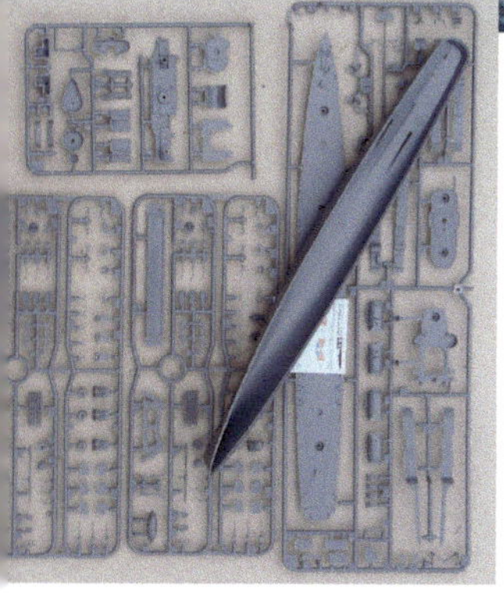

The box art is nicely done. It presents some drama and is a very realistic portrayal of the *Fletcher* in mid 1942. In the background is a *Sangamon* class escort carrier in an appropriate dapple camouflage and an *Omaha* class cruiser in a less appropriate splinter camouflage. The painting of the *Fletcher* is very realistic and can be used as a reference for superdetailing and rigging.

This kit can be built as full hull only. The hull is in one piece with a separate deck piece. The hull has delicate raised panel lines and a nice flare at the bow. However, the sheer line is not correct: there is a sharp break amidships rather than a graceful curve from stern to stem. This will be very difficult to correct.

The deckhouses are separate panels from the deck and are nicely detailed with all the doors and hatches in the correct place. These doors and portholes have 'eyebrows' above them but no detail on the door itself , but this can be remedied by attaching photo-etch doors.

As to the other parts, they are very nice. The whaleboats are a good shape and contain the correct arrangement of seats, etc. The 5in gunhouses come as five parts – base, two sides, gun barrel and top. There are all of the ladders and hatches moulded on to the sides and top. The gun barrel can be moved up and down within the house, which is always fun but it precludes the use of the blast bags which were always fitted over the gun barrel where it emerged from the gunhouse. Even worse, the gun barrel has a step in it whereas the real 5in/38 never did. Also the gunhouse is supposed to be somewhat off centre, with the slit for the gun barrel closer to the left of the gunhouse. This isn't the case in the kit. A less serious omission is the extra knuckle on the two maindeck gunhouses.

The 40mm twin looks good and to scale, as do the 20mm, but both would benefit from photo-etch gunsights and training wheels. The torpedo tubes again look good with the training equipment represented but a bit featureless.

The stacks are just about perfect and this is important, for they contribute as much as anything to the 'look' of a *Fletcher* class DD. The mast has a nice taper but is not correct for a *Fletcher* in 1942 (too many extrusions). This is easily dealt with using a razor blade or scalpel and the addition of photo-etch ladders and radar will improve matters immeasurably.

The other small parts are of a high standard. I especially like the side depth charge assemblage which correctly represents the depth charges mounted on pedestals. This whole area can be nicely detailed out of the box with a well-executed K-gun and loading crane. The rear depth charge racks are fine but the rack cage and the depth charges are moulded together. If one wanted to encase the row of depth charges in a photo-etch rack one would have an extremely difficult job removing the moulded-on rack cage.

The instructions are in well-written English, and one wonders why this wasn't the case for the 1/700 kit released at the same time. There is a painting diagram which accurately shows the complex splotch Measure 12 Mod camouflage that the *Fletcher* was painted after commissioning.

In summary this kit can be made into a decent replica of an early-war round-bridge *Fletcher* straight out of the box. It is also easily enhanced by photo-etch.

Trumpeter: *The Sullivans*, 1/350 scale

This kit can be built as a square-bridge *Fletcher* in a late-war configuration and there is a choice of full hull (a stand is included) or waterline. It is somewhat disappointing: although the basic shapes are correct, the quality of the moulds, parts and some design features are decidedly mediocre. There are imperfections found on a number of flat surfaces, and these will have to be sanded down.

The main deck is a separate part and shaped correctly, but the detail is poor. The anti-skid walkways are in relief and come out thick. These are normally painted on the deck and the walkway patterns are not all the same; it will be difficult to remove these. The anchor, chain locker, and capstan detail is over simplified. The anchor is not properly routed for the port side, but a solution would be to shave off the anchors completely and add real chain.

The deckhouses have a fair amount of detail – more so than the Tamiya kit, but it is not well executed. For example, the doors on the starboard deckhouse are heavier and more pronounced than portside. This will be very difficult to correct but it would be very easy to ignore in that on a fully assembled model only one set of doors can be viewed at any one time. They are also hinged incorrectly: on a ship the doors on the port side are hinged on the left; starboard doors are hinged on the right. This is done so that any waves that wash up over the deck will force the door closed and not open, preventing the ship from taking on excessive water. The stacks have nice pipework but are too slab-sided and the vents on the side are too thick and clumsy.

Although this kit has a number of flaws there are some things that are well very done.

To start with, the box art is very nice – a dramatic and well-executed picture of *The Sullivans* steaming through a rain squall. Likewise the 16-page instructions are well laid out and give enough information for superdetailing. The 5in gunhouses also measure up well. They have the correct offset and knuckles in the right places – as well as the different styles of gunhouses for the main and upper deck. However, there are several hatches that need to be added and one large one on the top that needs to be removed.

The K-guns are also well moulded, as are the side depth charges – except they are mounted on pedestals, as were all the early-war *Fletchers*, but pedestals never featured on a late-war *The Sullivans*.

So *The Sullivans* has lots of problems, but most of them minor and easily correctable. Many result from Trumpeter trying to go an extra step with regards to detail – such as the doors – and getting it wrong. Still, if one wants to put a bit of work in and perhaps cross it with the Tamiya *Fletcher* kit, one could produce a very nice late-war *Fletcher*.

Yankee Modelworks: *Fletcher*, *Stevens*, *Johnson* and *Kidd*, 1/350 scale

Master craftsman John Fickeln is responsible for the pattern and master for the *Fletcher*. The modifications for the other variants were done by another master, Mike Bishop. All four of these kits are of a very high quality but more expensive than the plastic kits in this scale. If one wants the highest quality and accuracy then these kits – with some cross kitting of the plastic *Fletchers* and aftermarket sets – are the way to go.

These kits are available from Yankee Modelworks and they are very well cast and detailed. The *Johnson* is the only mid-war kit available in this scale and the *Stevens* is the only catapult destroyer kit available in any scale.

(Lindberg): The Blue Devil DD, 1/125 scale

Named after the USS *Melvin* (DD 680), this kit has been on the market for over fifty years and if built out of the box it is really a motorised toy. It is included here because dedicated modellers have used it as a basis for a much better result by resorting to lots of scratch-building and modification of the original parts. Some nice models have been made using this approach, but one is reminded of the story of the axe: 'It turned out to be a very good axe after I replaced the blade and then replaced the handle.' The primary virtue of this kit is that it is large and inexpensive.

Accessories

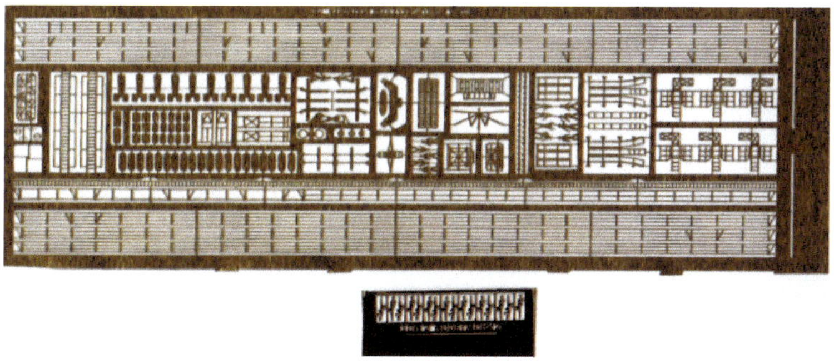

Toms Modelworks: Destroyer photo-etch set, 1/700 scale

Toms DD set is a venerable offering, one of the original PE sets for waterline ships. It has railings, depth charge racks for the side and rear and storage racks as well, radars, doors hatches, railings, life raft supports, VHF antennas and 20mm Oerlikon shields and pedestals. There are even some PE figures to crew the destroyer. Almost all these parts are useable; however, the railings are over-scale.

Gold Medal Models: Cruiser/Destroyer photo-etch set, 1/700 scale

Another PE set that been around for a long time. This set has been recently upgraded to include some new, and very nice items. Like the Toms Modelworks set it includes railings, depth charge racks for the side and rear and storage racks as well, radars, doors hatches, railings, life raft supports, VHF antennas. In addition it includes whaleboat rudders, funnel grilles, yardarms and some lovely lifeboat davits – the only thing in scale

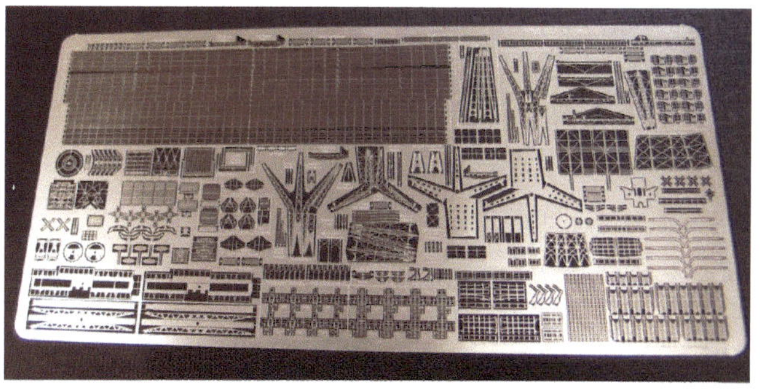

for this item. The same applies for depth charge cranes. There are also some PE fighting lights which will look very nice and to scale.

Pitroad: Equipment for US Navy Ships, 1/700 scale, Set E6

Pitroad (Skywave) provides a series of aftermarket plastic kits of parts. This one, E6, has the most appropriate set of replacement parts for 1/700 *Fletcher* DD sets. This set has 5in gunhouses – no offset or extra knuckles and missing some hatches, but otherwise to scale and sharp looking. It also has 5in gun barrels with blast bags, 40mm weapons far superior to the ones in the kits above (except Trumpeter), liferafts, Mk 51 AA gun directors, Mk 37 5in gun director, 24in and 36in searchlights, depth charge cranes and side racks with K-gun assembly, 26ft whaleboats and other items of generally better quality than the parts found in the kits.

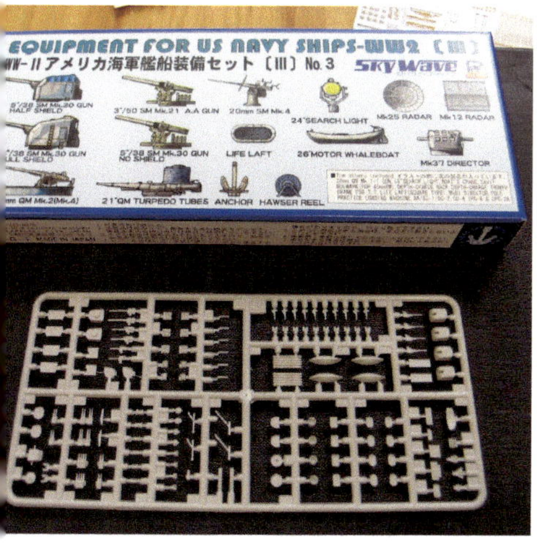

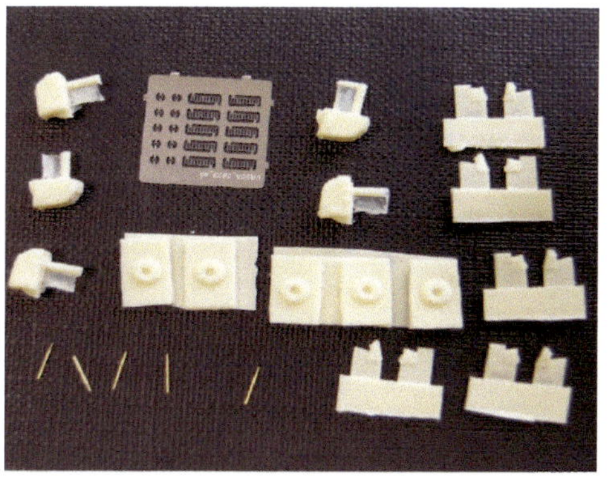

Voyager: 5in 38cal Weapons, 1/700 scale

This is the ultimate solution to the 5in weapons on a *Fletcher* DD. This set includes five resin gunhouses, with the right number of hatches in the correct place and the offset of the gunhouse correct. There is also a resin blast bag and turret ring and a brass 5in gun barrel. They come in two sets, one with the extra knuckle for the maindeck gunhouses.

Toms Modelworks: *Fletcher* detail photo-etch set, 1/350 scale

This set has been designed specifically to enhance the Tamiya *Fletcher* kit. It has railings, depth charge racks for the side and rear and storage racks as well, radars, doors hatches, railings, life raft supports, mesh for the bottom of liferafts, floater nets, VHF antennas and funnel grilles. A nice addition is the side bulwark with limber holes and doorway.

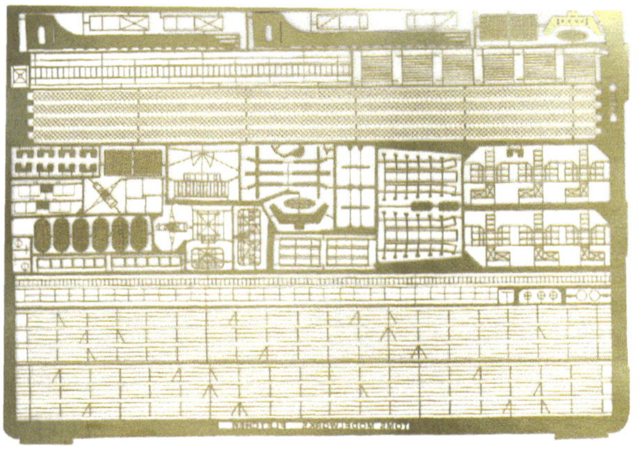

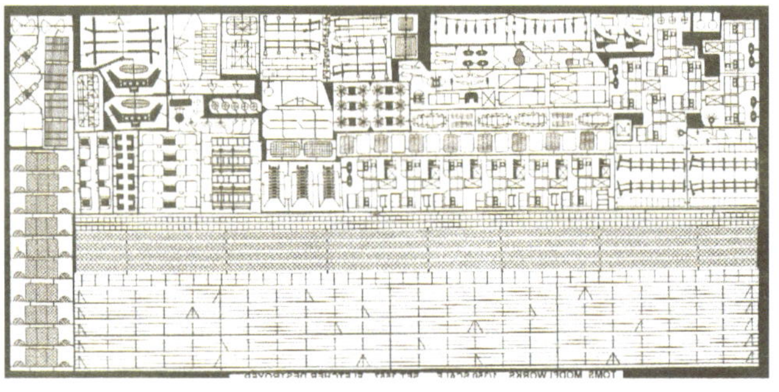

Toms Modelworks: *The Sullivans* detail photo-etch set, 1/350 scale

This set is for the Trumpeter *The Sullivans* kit and is a newer, more complete set than the *Fletcher* set described above, but there are some interesting omissions and additions. The side bulwark is gone as are the raft bottoms. There is a lot of new stuff such as railings for 40mm weapons, rudders and propellers for the whaleboats, cable reels, mast detail and platforms. Especially nice are the lifelines that are rigged above the whaleboat.

Gold Medal Models: *Fletcher* detail photo-etch set, 1/350 scale

This is a large set designed specifically for *Fletcher* class destroyers and parts for early and late-war models. It is a large set with the expected railings, depth charge racks for the side and rear and storage racks as well, radars, doors hatches, railings, liferaft supports, mesh for the bottom of liferafts, floater nets, VHF antennas and funnel grilles. The railings have cut-outs for chocks and other deck-edge obstructions that will be very handy. There is also detailing parts for 40mm and 20mm AA weapons. A special bonus is the assortment of relief etched doors and hatches, especially tailored for the Tamiya 1/350 kit which lacks door details this fine.

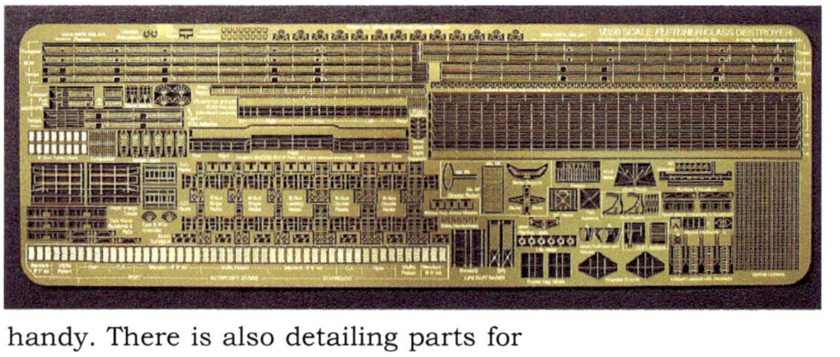

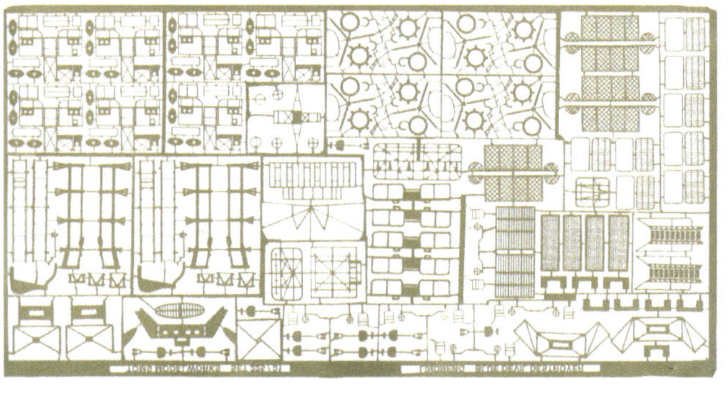

TMM: *Blue Devil* detail set, 1/125 scale

This kit is basically an enlarged 1/350 scale set but will be essential for anybody trying to make a decent model of the Lindberg *Blue Devil* DD. Particularly useful will be the AA detail parts with gunsights, training wheels, rails, shoulder brackets, seats with pedals for the guncrew. There is a separate sprue consisting entirely of railings and mesh for the forward main deck railings.

Summary of *Fletcher* Class Kits

Scale	Company	Kit	Comments
1/96	Deans Marine	*Fletchers*	For advanced modellers
1/96	Scale Shipyard	*Fletchers*	For advanced modellers
1/48	Scale Shipyard	*Fletchers*	For advanced modellers
1/125	Lindberg	Blue Devil / *Melvin*	Motorised. Has many inaccuracies
1/192	Bluejacket	*Fletchers*	Craftsman kit
1/192	Iron Shipwright	*Fletcher* Class	Limited edition
1/305	Revell	*Fletchers*	Post-war ASW fit with Hedgehog in place of No 2 5in mount
1/305	Revell	*Radford*	Post-war ASW fit with Hedgehog in place of No 2 5in mount
1/305	Revell	*The Sullivans*	Post-war ASW fit with Hedgehog in place of No 2 5in mount
1/305	Revell	*Zerstorer Z1*	Post-war ASW fit with Hedgehog in place of No 2 5in mount
1/350	Tamiya	*Fletchers*	Early-war *Fletchers*
1/350	Trumpeter	*The Sullivans*	Late-war configuration
1/350	Yankee MW	*Fletchers*	Originally BWN
1/350	Yankee MW	*Stevens*	Catapult version
1/350	Yankee MW	*Johnson*	Originally BWN, mid-war square-bridge
1/350	Yankee MW	*Kidd*	Originally BWN late-war?
1/509	Aurora	*Bennion*	Long out of production. Average quality and accuracy
1/600	Aurora	*Halford*	OOP. Inaccurate model of floatplane conversion. Has a *Gearing* style bridge!
1/670	Hawk	WWII Destroyer	Box art shows *The Sullivans*. Re-issued by Testors
1/700	Matchbox	*Fletchers*	Low quality but good shape
1/700	Skywave	*Fletcher* Class	Two in box
1/700	Skywave	*Callaghan*	
1/700	Tamiya	*Fletcher*	
1/700	Tamiya	*Cushing*	
1/700	Trumpeter	*The Sullivans*	
1/700	Samek	*The Sullivans*	
1/700	BSW	*Fletchers*	

Modelmakers' Showcase

Halford 1943 scratch-built by Joseph Neumeyer, 1/96 scale

This exciting 1/96 scale model was constructed by Joseph Neumeyer of Dynamic Dioramas. It shows one of the three *Fletcher* Class DDs that were modified to have a catapult on the aft deckhouse. Joseph made this model as a commission for a client who wanted it as a display for his shop in Montrose, California. Joseph has been interested in modelling – especially dioramas – since he was a youngster in Hancock Park.

This one is of the *Halford* when she had a catapult fitted. Six *Fletcher* class destroyers were selected for an experimental conversion (DDs 476-481), but only three – *Pringle*, *Stevens* and *Halford* were actually completed as such. In any event, the experiment did not work out and all three destroyers were re-converted to the normal mid-war *Fletcher* configuration and served honourably for the rest of the war.

Although there is plentiful data on *Fletcher* class destroyers, specialised information on the three catapult destroyers is an exception. The client provided ships' logs, while Floating Drydock provided plans and pictures. The crane on the starboard side was the hard part – there was only a plan view and a few pictures. By educated guesses and studying other similar cranes of the USN, Joseph was able to construct an accurate replica. This was borne out by a letter that the owner of the model received from a crewmember of the *Halford*. In this letter the sailor states how moved he was to see such a lovingly made replica of his own ship, and remarked on the accuracy of the aircraft-handling crane as it was his job to operate that crane.

The hull of this ship was a standard fibreglass *Fletcher* hull from Scale Shipyard of Long Beach, California. They also supplied the deck guns and other standard fittings, such as cable reels and torpedo tubes. These basic details were considerably enhanced by scratch-building extra features. For instance, the torpedo tubes had various rods, cylinders, training wheels, and other detail added to the basic forms supplied by the manufacturer.

A number of parts were derived from other kits and modified to suit. This method of modelmaking is a technique known as 'kit-bashing'. Often the actual model part would bear no relationship to what it was used on the *Halford* model but it had a similar shape or complexity to what was needed. The idea was to accurately 'indicate' rather than exactly 'reproduce' the form being modelled.

For those who wish to see this model, it is on display at Collector's World, located at 2249 Honolulu Avenue, Montrose, California 91020.

A dramatic picture of Joseph Neumeyer's model of the *Halford*. Note how the drama and excitement is increased by having all of the guns and radar trained at the same target above.

Above: This shows the positioning and type of catapult used on the *Halford*. The catapult was made from a photo-etch set as a cut down cruiser-type catapult.

Right: This picture shows how Joseph scratch-built or kit-bashed lots of small items to give the necessary realism. An example would be the siren atop the fore stack.

Left: A view of the bridge and the activity around it. The scene is brought to life by the addition of figures in action poses and details such as empty shell cases scattered behind the gunhouse.

Below: This is a view of the specialised crane installed to retrieve the aircraft out of the water. In the absence of close-up photos this can serve as a good reference for model-builders.

Above: At 1/96 scale the Kingfisher is a work of art in itself. Also all of the scratch-built 'clutter' attached to the bulkheads is nicely visible.

Right: Torpedo tubes were built up from basic parts supplied by Scale Shipyard to get the level of detail needed to match the rest of the ship.

Above: A good view of how the aft 40mm gun tub nestled in between the depth charge racks. Note the teardrop shape of the tub which contains both the 40mm twin and the Mk 51 director.

Below: A dramatic angle of the *Halford* at action stations cutting through the water.

Tamiya *Charles Ausburne* 1942 and 1944 by Loren Perry, 1/350 scale

Loren Perry's name is well known to many modellers through his company Gold Medal Models. He has been making models since he was seven years old when his father, who was with the US Coast Guard, one day brought home the Lindberg kit of an LST. This got Loren started and he has never really stopped.

Loren's company, Gold Medal Models, provides aftermarket accessories to the model industry, primarily photo-etch but GMM also produces a range of decals. Loren's company was founded in 1985 and is considered the grandfather of all PE and aftermarket companies. Loren used photo-etch techniques previously for his own models – including a Gold Medal prize-winner. So impressed were the observers he was asked to produce some extra sets for a hobby shop. He did a run of twenty, expecting that the stock would last for a year or so. Much to his surprise the shop called within two days asking for twenty more. The whole thing took off from there and within four years Gold Medal Models was Loren's fulltime job. Since then he has gone from strength to strength producing top quality photo-etch sets for ships of all scales.

Loren chose the *Charles Ausburne* because of her history as the flagship of Arleigh '31 Knot' Burke and his famous DesRon 23, the 'Little Beavers'. His primary purpose was to demonstrate the GMM 350-14 *Fletcher* class destroyer kit set. The skill that has won him many prizes and love of modelling made sure that the models were classics. To research his two *Charles Ausburnes* Loren used a planbook for *Fletcher* class destroyers, a Morskie Profile publication and he also used the considerable research that Tamiya put in the model itself.

Loren used stock parts for both these models. The purpose of this was to show just how a prize-winning model could be made out of the box with only the addition of the GMM 350-14 PE set. Of course there was some scratch-building required – especially for the late-war where sponsons for the extra 40mm and other major modifications that were not in the kit – which represented an early-war *Fletcher*. One may also see little additions such as the ship's siren and platform on the forward stack, fighting lights and other touches that give these models that extra realism not found in the stock parts. The model is also rigged, and for this Loren used .002in fly tippit for the halyards and antenna wires and .003in for standing rigging.

Below: The *Charles Ausburne* in her 1944 configuration. The 1/350 Tamiya kit was the basis, but it needed some scratch-building to add the sponsons for the 40mm twins, Mk 51 directors on the stacks and atop the pilothouse, and the 20mm on the fantail. The same photo-etch set was used, demonstrating that it could be applied for both early- and late-war *Fletcher* class DDs.

Above: The *Charles Ausburne* in her early-war configuration. The 1/350 Tamiya kit was the basis: it was made straight out of the box with the addition of GMM photo-etch set of aftermarket parts.

Above: A view of the fantails of both models showing the early-war and late-war configurations. Note the addition of storage racks for the depth charges in the late-war version.

Right: Another nice comparison of the early- and later-war configurations of the same ship. While the major changes of AA armament are clearly visible, one can note subtle changes such as the stretchers on the bulkhead of the late-war version and the presence of additional liferafts,

Above: A nice close-up of the bridge on the late-war *Charles Ausburne*. It shows the placement of the navigation lights (red for port) and forward Mk 51 directors. Note how the ladders are not glued flat on the bulkhead: rather the ends are turned in to give some space between the latter and bulkhead, as it was in the real ship.

Above: This close up of the early-war *Charles Ausburne* shows some interesting scratch-built, PE and rigging detail. Note the ship's siren and platform on the stack. One can also see how the signal halyards were fastened adjacent to the flag lockers. The canvas screens on the searchlight platforms are made from the PE set, as is the stretcher visible on the bulkhead at the bottom left of the picture.

Below: This close up of the late-war *Charles Ausburne* shows Loren's meticulous workmanship on a smaller scale model. In the late-war *Fletchers* the depth charges were double racked alongside the K-gun.

Kidd 1945 scratch-built by Don Pruel, 1/192 scale

Don is a well-known professional modeller. Some of his most famous models are the *Akagi* and now the *Arizona* at the Pearl Harbor memorial. This model of the *Kidd* was built, like most of Don's work, for a private collector.

Don is from the Chesapeake Bay area. He has been interested in modelling from his early years; his father and brother were also avid modellers and became his mentors.

Above: This prize-winning model reflects the *Kidd* as she is today – and as she was in late-1945. The *Kidd* is preserved as a museum ship at Baton Rouge, Louisiana and as such has been restored as closely as possible to her 1945 appearance.

His first job as a professional modeller was working on the models at the Naval Academy at Annapolis, and it would be difficult to imagine a better place to start. Prior to that he had worked as an aircraft mechanic, auto mechanic and owned his own business as an automobile bodywork and paint technician. These jobs were a good training ground for his career as a modeller and owner manager of a modelling business.

Don is passionate about modelling, and rightfully considers all of his models works of art with personal rewards beyond the commercial. Don relates that when his model of the *Akagi* was unveiled at the Pearl Harbor museum an invited guest was a Japanese pilot who flew from the carrier during the infamous attack. The pilot studied the model of the *Akagi* for a very long time and with moist eyes muttered something in Japanese. Don asked for it to be translated – the pilot said 'that was just how it was'.

This brilliant model was built in an incredibly short span of 30 days – even more unbelievable in that *everything* (with the exception of the anchor chains) was scratch-built. There is a 1/1 example of the *Kidd* in Baton Rouge. Don, however, is located in a prime area for research. He lives in Annapolis near the Naval Academy library, and is also an hour away from the National Archives. With such bountiful resources nearby he did not need to visit, but he was greatly assisted by the *Kidd* Foundation, as well as by a photography expedition by a friend to get specific details that were unclear from the other reference sources.

Don uses traditional scratch-building techniques – *everything* is fashioned directly from raw materials such as pewter, resin, wood and styrene. The only bought part in this model is the anchor chain. The hull is first hand carved in basswood, a mould is taken and then resin is poured in. Small parts such as weapons, searchlights, etc are made from cast lead-free pewter with brass wire, styrene, and photo-etch to enhance detail.

Looking at the detail in all the components, one might despair of ever completing a model like this. Many of these components, however, come from Don's parts box. His favoured scale is 1/192 and although all the parts are cast from masters made by Don himself, over the years he has built up a virtual ordinance depot of 1/192 naval weapons and fittings. This is one way in which he can complete a fantastically detailed 1/192 model of a USN subject in such a short time and yet claim that it was all 'scratch-built'.

Even with the luxury of a large selection of weapons and fittings it is not all plain sailing. For example, the radar assembly atop the mast was made up of no less than forty separate pieces of photo-etch parts, resin and pewter to give the accuracy required for this model. For the rigging Don used fine silk thread, varying the thickness and colouring according to the rigging usage: running rigging light colour; standing rigging thicker and black; thin black for antenna wires.

Right: The anchor chains are the only thing not scratch-built on this model.

Below: Don's workmanship is crisp and fresh. This model has the pristine 'just out of the dockyard' feel to it.

Below: This shows the double-racked depth charge arrangement installed on all destroyers modified late in the war.

Right: Fantastic detail is present on the Mk 37 5in gun director. Other bridge fittings such as signalling lamps and observation positions are also visible.

Left: The midships area is crammed with scratch-built detail. Note how the use of colour highlights items such as hose reels, fire extinguishers, etc. There is also a good view of twin 20mm – these did not appear on the *Fletchers* until mid-1945.

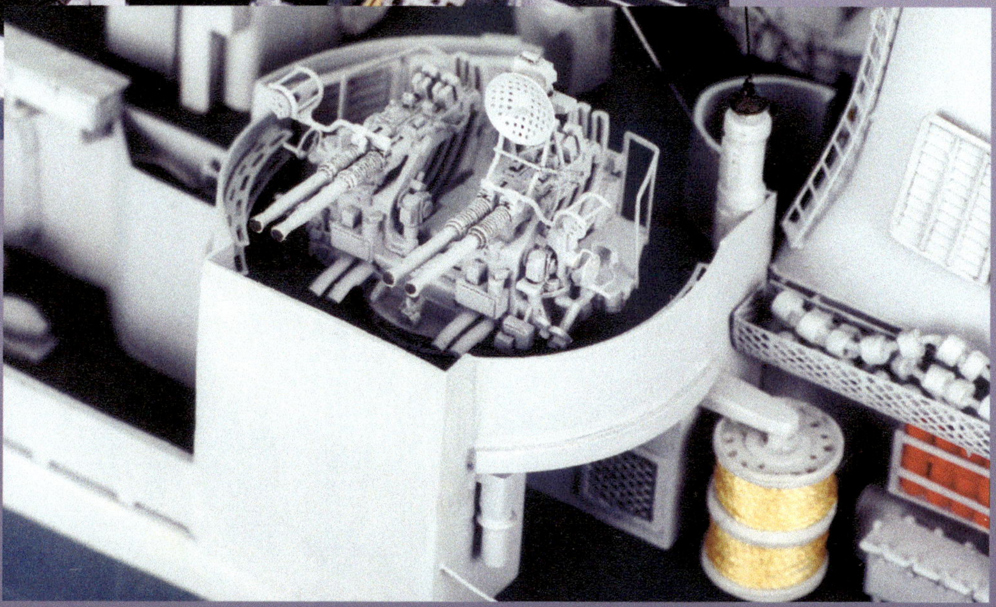

Right: The quad 40mm comes from Don's own personal 1/192 weapons depot. With this arsenal he can add fantastic and accurate detail without stretching out building time.

Left: A view of one of the more obscure areas of a destroyer, the back of the bridge. One can see the locations of the ship's ladders, the ship's bell and the painting that adorned the *Kidd*'s stack throughout the war. Although she was named after Admiral Kidd who died at Pearl Harbor, she was known by her crew as 'The Pirate of the Pacific', invoking images of the swashbuckling pirate Captain Kidd.

Below: Another product of Don's miniature arsenal, the ubiquitous single 5in/ 38 gunhouse. Note the placement of handholds, hatches as well as the sighting hood.

Left: The SC-2 radar aerial took forty separate pieces to build. This also gives a good view of the radio antenna suite and the position of the fighting lights in a late-war configuration.

Right: One can see the different types of rigging material in this photo. At this scale it is just possible to depict the rigging halyards correctly – a double strand through a block.

Below: The ultimate modeller's reference – the ship herself. *Kidd* at Baton Rouge, Louisiana. Other preserved *Fletchers* include the *Cassin Young* at Boston, Massachusetts, and *The Sullivans* at Buffalo, New York.

Kidd present day, 1/1 scale

Anyone wanting to build a model of a *Fletcher* is lucky to have full-size reference in the form of a number of preserved museum ships. Although most represent the ship's appearance at the end of the war (often with some later features), many of the weapons and fittings are typical. The following selection of photos was taken aboard USS *Kidd* at Baton Rouge, Louisiana, and all are reproduced by courtesy of SeaPhoto – www.warshipphotos.com.

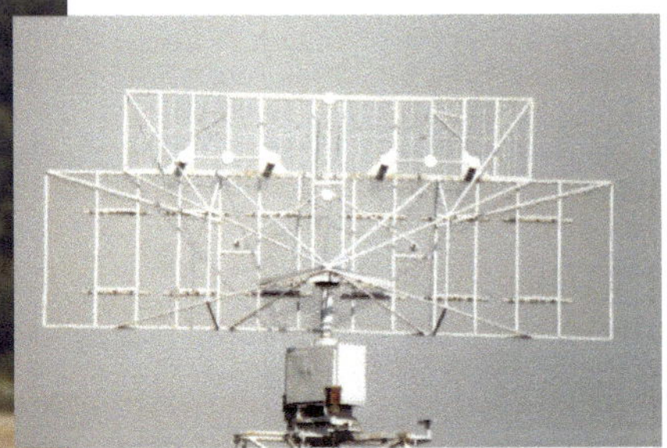

Fletcher 1942, Measure 12 Mod

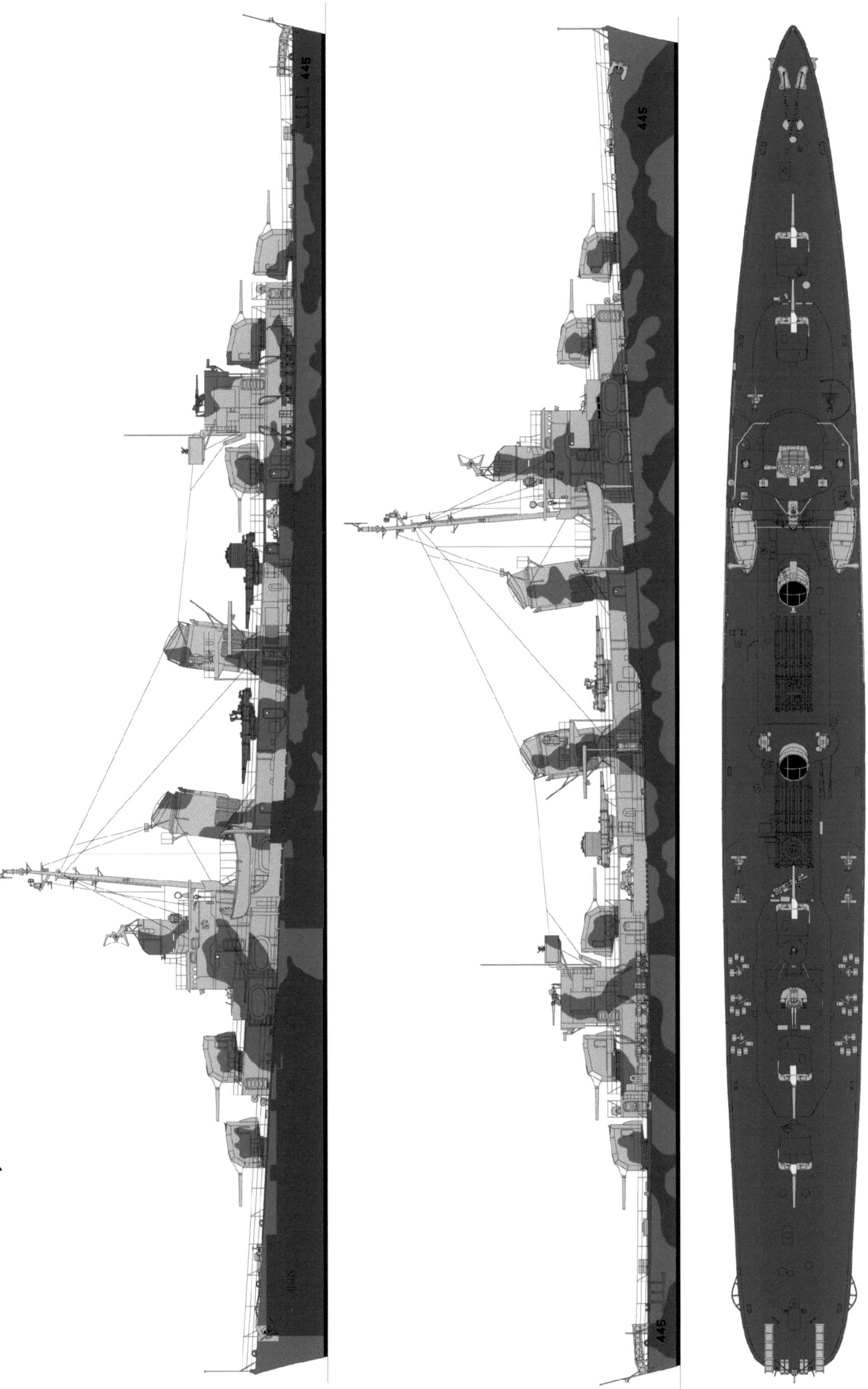

Stevens 1943, Measure 21

Hoel 1944, Measure 31/1D

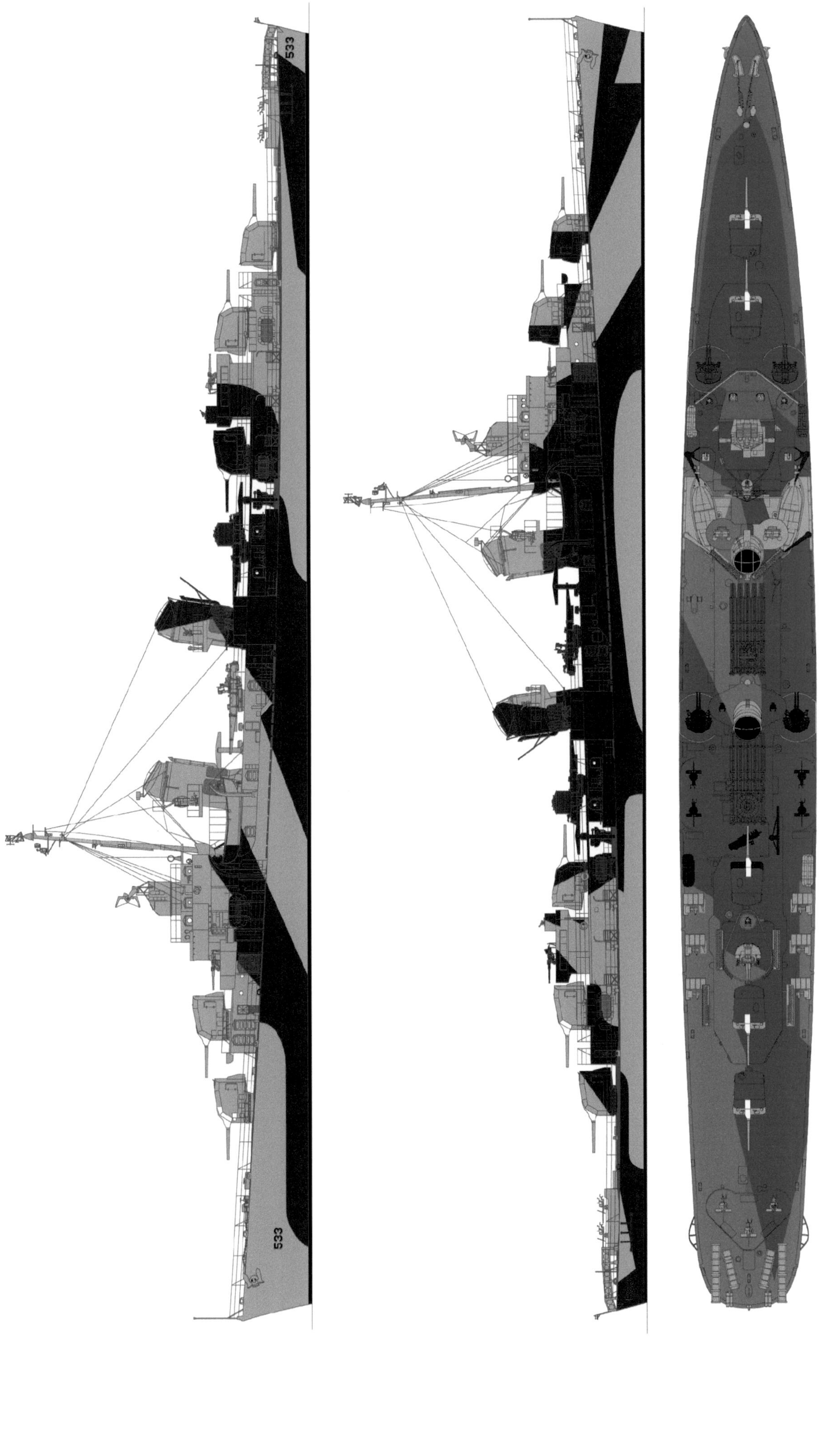

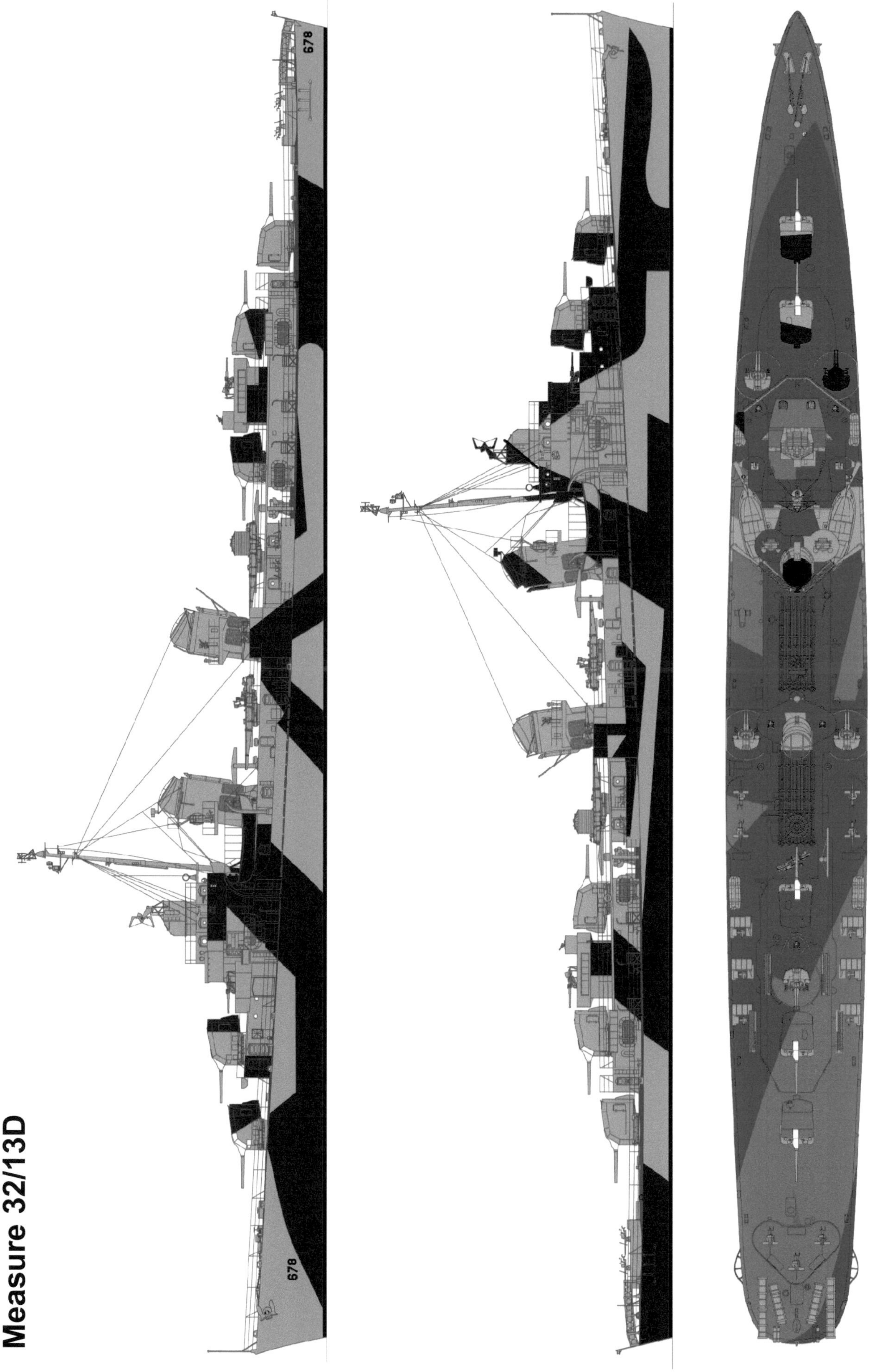

***McGowan* 1944, Measure 32/13D**

Charles Ausburne 1944, Measure 32/14D

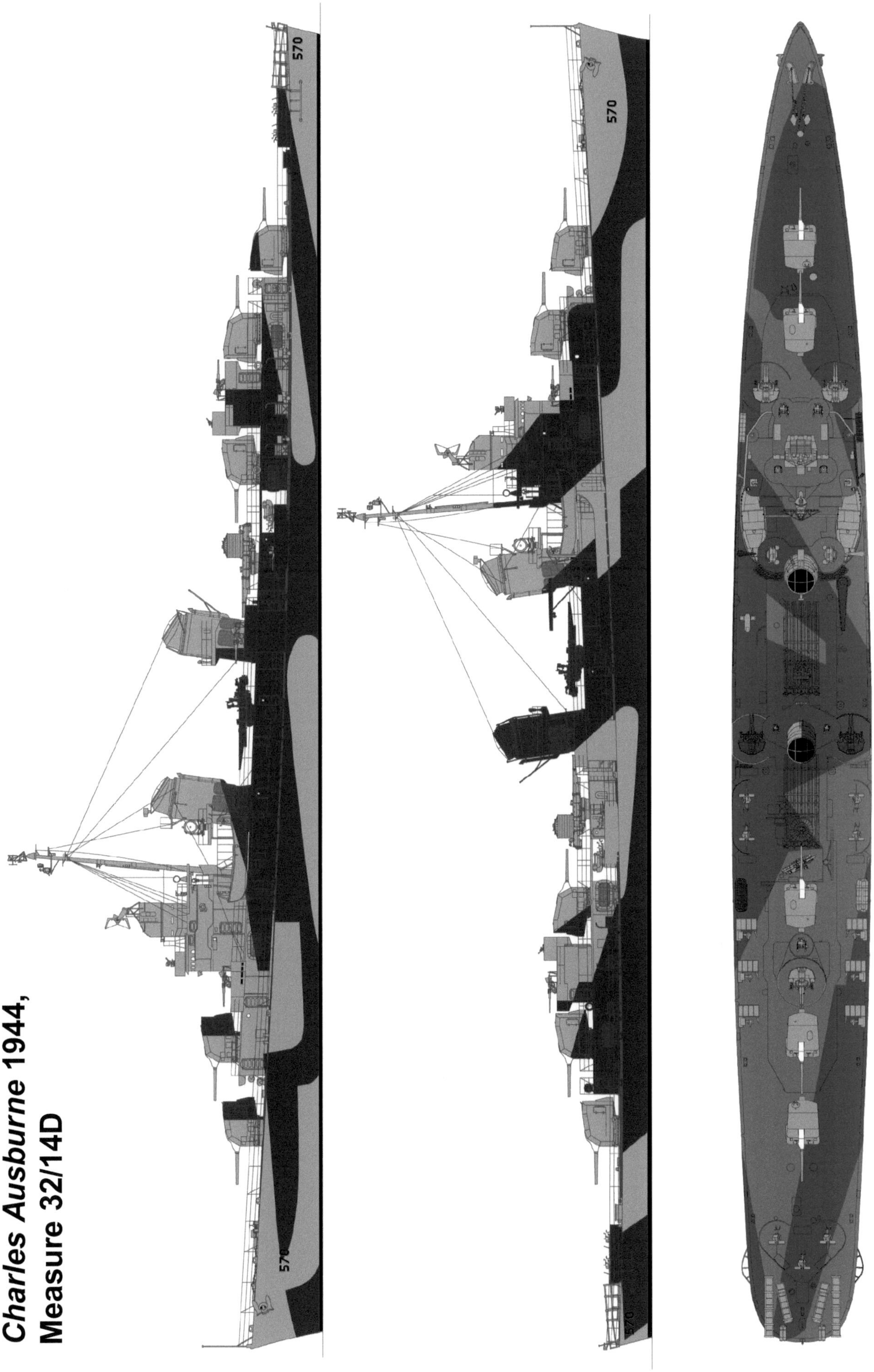

Stoddard 1944, Measure 32/16D

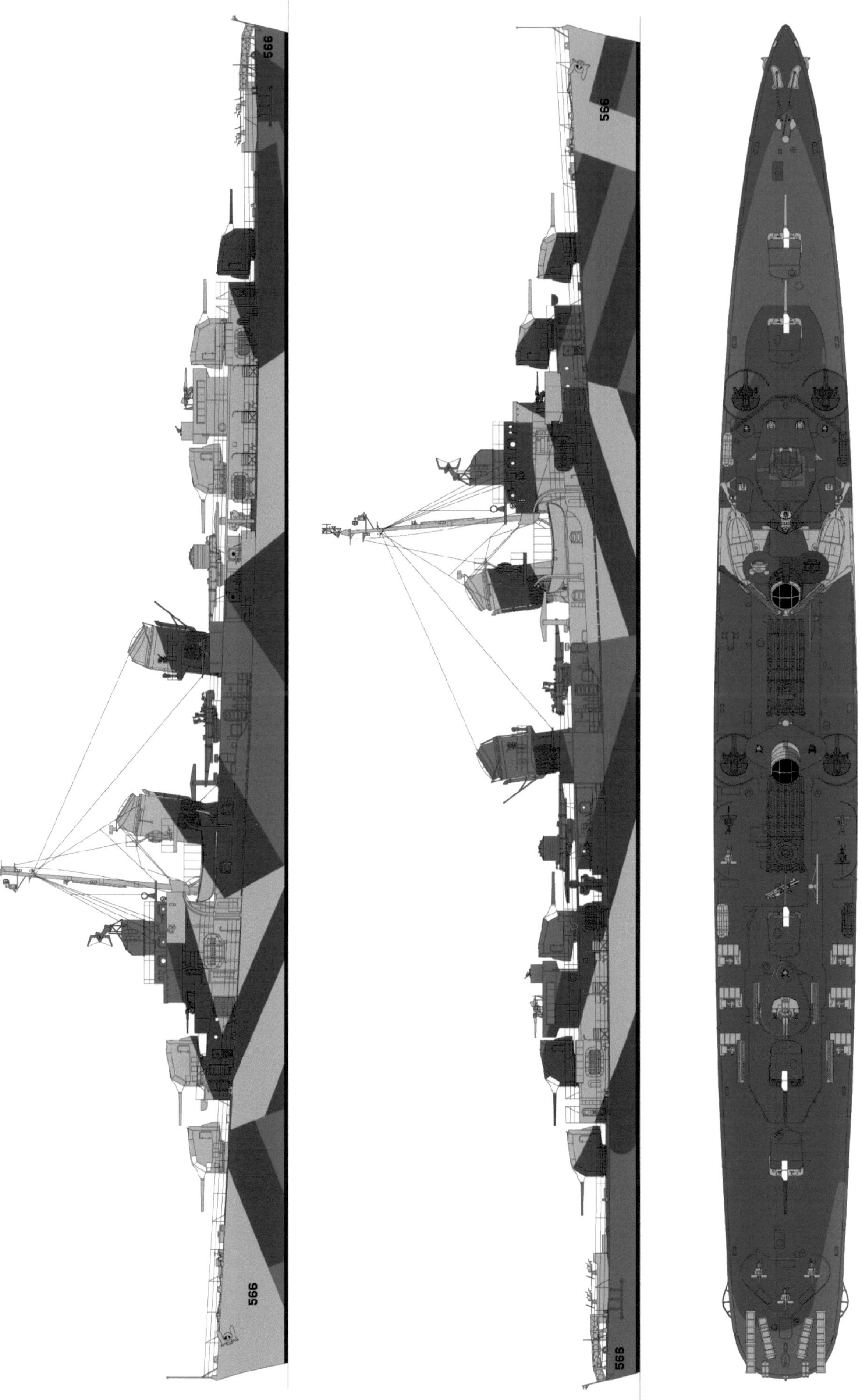

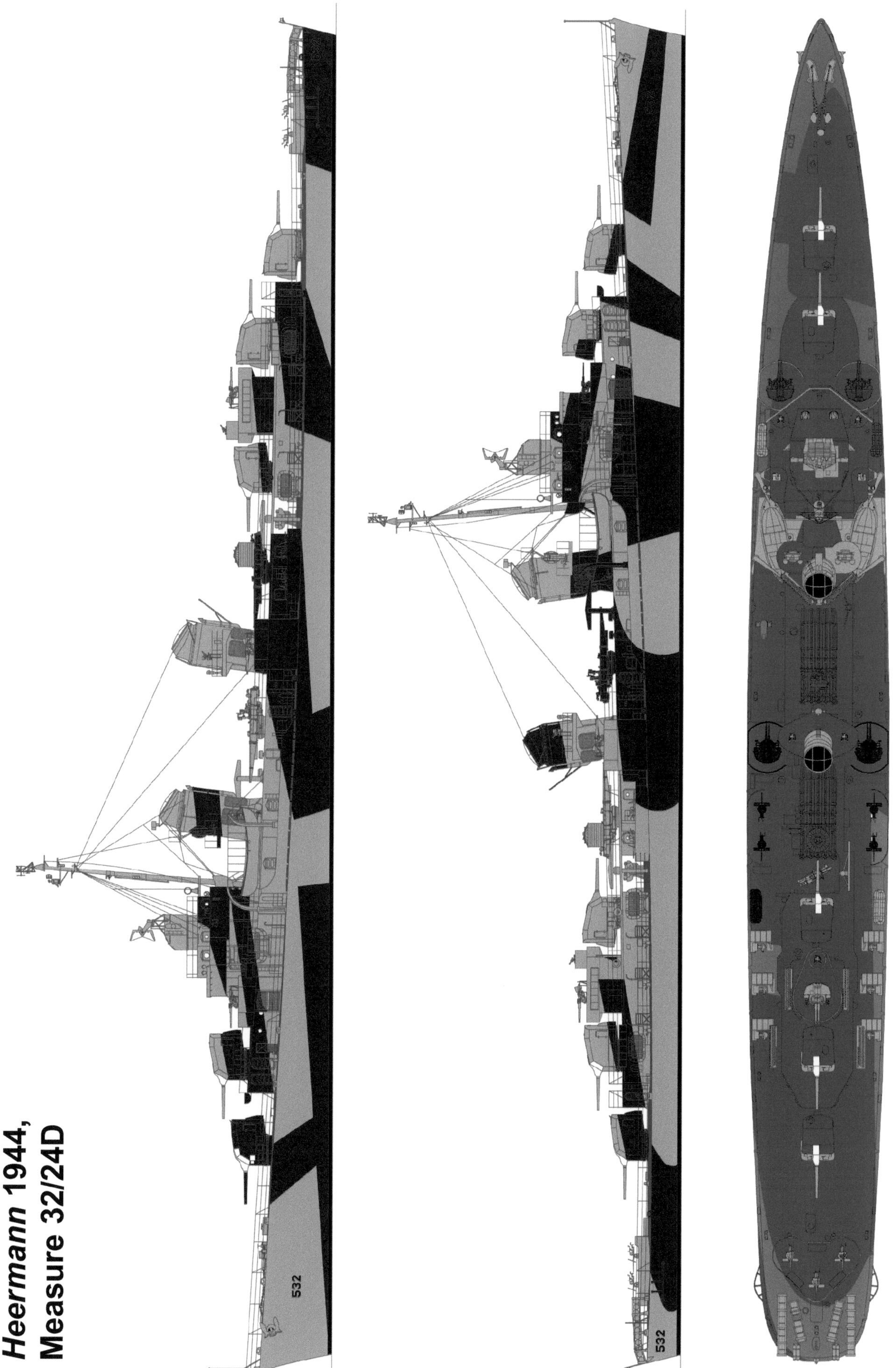

Heermann 1944, Measure 32/24D

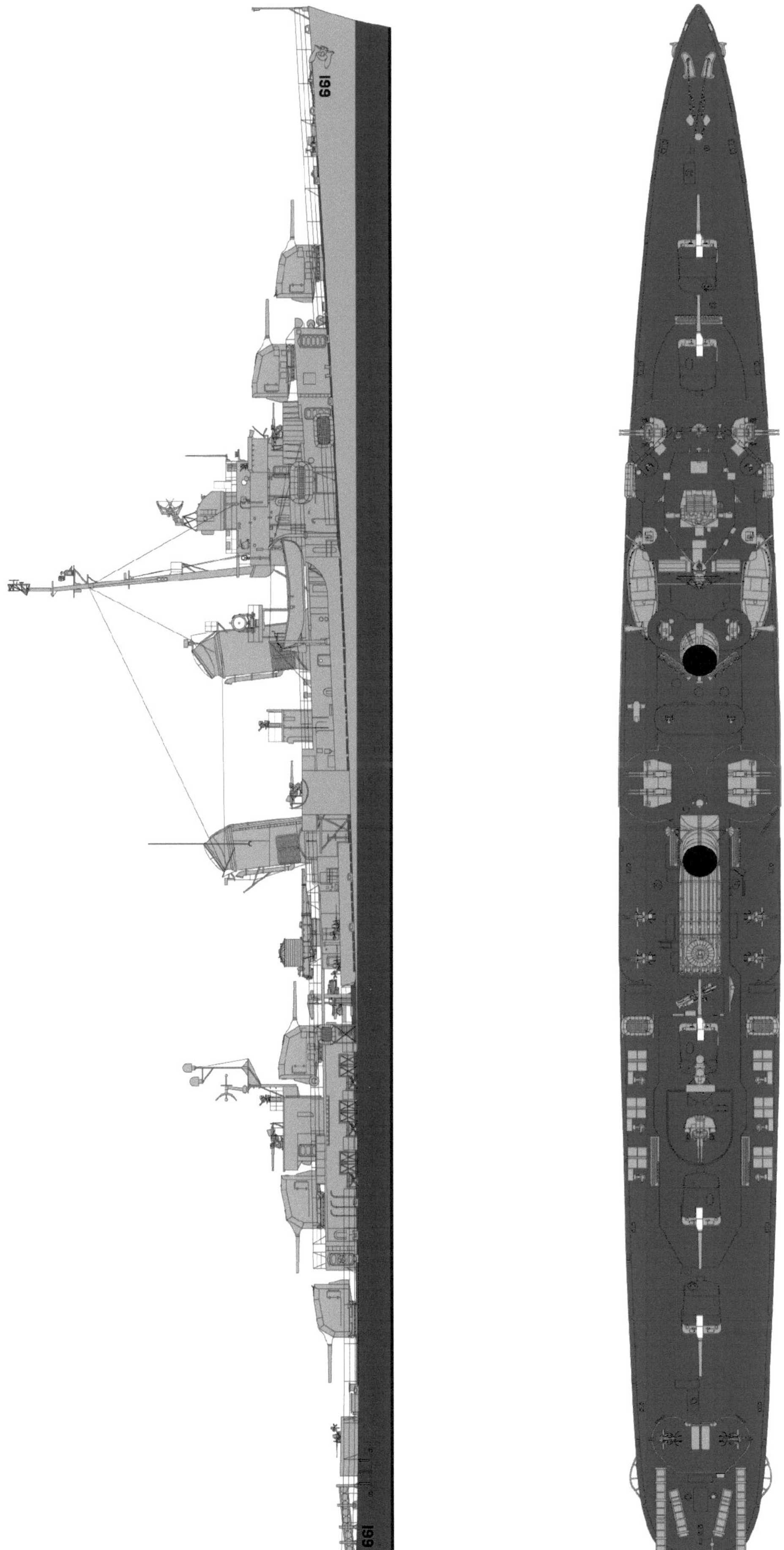

***Kidd* 1945, Measure 22**

Appearance

The *Fletcher* and her classmates were handsome ships. Long, low-slung, with raked stacks and foremast, they had a graceful but purposeful look to them. They have become the archetypal 'destroyer' profile of that era. The ships were well proportioned – a flush deck with a graceful sheer, three deckhouses, two raked stacks (larger than the previous classes but not overly thick) and five 5in 38cal weapons prominently visible on the centreline.

Given that 175 *Fletcher* class destroyers were built and most were later modified, there is a considerable variety in appearance – in armament configuration, camouflage scheme and superstructure. Fortunately, the above can be considered as indices in a matrix and any particular *Fletcher* class destroyer's appearance can be described within those parameters. For example, the destroyer *Claxton* in 1943 could be described as round-bridge, early-war armament, wearing Measure 21 camouflage.

Below:The *Chevalier* (DD 451) on 24 October 1942, one of the three *Fletchers* that went to combat with 1.1in quads. In this photo they are covered atop the aft deckhouse between 5in mounts Nos 3 and 4. (USN).

LaVallette (DD 448) on 8 October 1942, showing the early form of two-level after platform for the twin 40mm Bofors just forward of No 4 5in gun. This ship also has a twin 40mm on the fantail. (USN)

These are the major variants.

SUPERSTRUCTURE

The *Fletcher* class can be considered as two subclasses – round bridge and square bridge. The initial design was for a rounded bridge and pilothouse and can be found on the first 58 ships: (DDs 445-451, 465-481, 499-502, 507-517, 550-553,569-580, 592-593). The bridge and pilothouse were a two-level composite structure rounded in front with bridge wings protruding just abaft the rounded part of the bridge. The Mk 37 5in gun director was mounted on a 10ft (3.05m) pedestal atop the bridge to give maximum visibility. After the design, but prior to commissioning, Mk 12 fire control radar was added on top of the gun director. As fire control radar and additional AA armament was added (even prior to commissioning) this design became top-heavy and the curved bridge took up valuable construction time.

The *Fletcher* as launched mounted five 5in/38s, a quad 1.1in AA and four 20mm guns. The torpedo armament consisted of ten 21in tubes in two quintuple mounts. The aft torpedo mount had a small circular structure over the training apparatus to protect it from the blast from the No 3 5in gun (it was called the 'doghouse' by the crewmen). The depth charge armament consisted of six K-guns and storage racks and two roller racks over the fantail. In the early part of the war the depth charges in the waist were mounted on pedestals (four per K-gun), later they were mounted on small racks enclosed in cages and by the end of the war they were in double racks (enclosed in cages) per K-gun.

Halfway up the aft stack was a searchlight platform with two 36in searchlights.

While fitting out, the 1.1in quad was replaced by a 40mm twin. This happened in almost all of the early *Fletchers* with the exception of the *Nicholas*, *O'Bannon* and *Chevalier*, which went to the combat zones in the Solomon Islands with the 1.1in quads.

To make things more complex the first seven round-bridge destroyers (DD 445-451) had a raised, two-level platform for the 40mm and director atop the deckhouse that was between the third and fourth 5in gunhouses. All subsequent ships had a lower platform with a single level 'teardrop' shaped gun tub for a twin 40mm and director in the same tub. The Mk 51 (Mk 49 on the earlier *Fletchers*) director was forward of the twin 40mm in the narrow end of the teardrop.

As for the rest of the AA armament there was again some variety. The *Fletcher* design called for two 20mm cannons mounted in the waist and two more mounted on the deck just behind the second 5in gun. Before commissioning an extra two 20mm located right next to the original two in the waist were added. This brought the total to six 20mm cannons. Some of the destroyers had two or three 20mm cannons mounted on the fantail while others had a 40mm twin mounted there.

Other variations of AA armament on

This picture of the *Thatcher* (DD 514) shows the places about the forward superstructure where 20mm cannons were mounted – on top of the pilothouse, and also on a platform sponsoned out from the front of the bridge. Note the 40mm twin on the fantail and the Mk 49 director on the aft deckhouse. (USN)

Right: The *Halford* underway in April 1943. The position of the catapult is clearly visible. On the fantail is a twin 40mm mount and adjacent to the aft stack the primitive crane arrangement can be discerned. (USN)

Right: One of the catapult destroyers, USS *Pringle* (DD 477) on 25 April 1943 after reconversion to a five-gun destroyer. Note the absence of superstructure between Nos 3 and 4 gunhouses, the single 20mm guns being mounted directly on the 01 deck level. However, there are full width sponsons abreast the aft stack for twin 40mm Bofors. (USN)

the early round-bridge *Fletchers* were the addition of extra 20mm atop the bridge or directly in front of it. A few had both.

The most startling appearance variation was for the six catapult destroyers (DD 476-481). They had the deckhouse between guns 4 and 5 completely removed as well as gunhouse No 3 and the torpedo tubes just forward of them. This made room for a catapult of the cruiser type, but lightened by removing the catwalks and rails that normally surrounded them. These striking looking ships (all round-bridge DDs) never used their aircraft in combat as the experiment was considered a failure. The catapults were removed and the gunhouse, deckhouse and torpedo armament were restored

Right: This picture of the *Benham* (DD 796) in January 1944 gives a clear view of the bridge arrangement and the placement of the added AA armament, although the 40mm twins are all covered by canvas. (USN)

prior to entering the combat zone.

To reduce construction complexity and to reduce topweight, a 'square-bridge' build was introduced on the DD 518, USS *Brownson.* The hull and most of the superstructure was identical to the early *Fletchers* but the bridge area and armament were different. The square-bridge configuration differed in that the pilothouse and bridge were no longer a monolithic two-level structure on the forward deckhouse. Now the lower level was squared and projected further forward and the pilothouse on top was smaller. The bridge wings expanded to become a platform that extended entirely around the pilothouse. The elegant rounded face of the original *Fletchers'* bridge was replaced with square bulkheads and a more pyramidal look. In addition, the pedestal for the Mk 37 gun director was lowered by 6ft, thereby saving top-weight which was needed for the ever-increasing number of AA weapons mounted.

Another significant difference was the AA armament: the middle deckhouse grew some sponsons adjacent to the aft stack. These sponsons were the full width of the hull. These were needed for two more 40mm twins. The searchlights on the aft stack were replaced by Mk 51 directors and the searchlight platform was moved to the forward stack. The 20mm singles on the forward deckhouse were replaced by a larger gun tub with 40mm twins. On the fantail between the depth charge racks was another gun tub with two or three 20mm. This brought the total armament to ten 40mm and seven 20mm. This in effect became the standard and there was much less variation as commissioned than in the round-bridge DDs.

A dockyard photo taken on 2 July 1945 of the *Howorth* (DD 592) demonstrating the enhanced AA fit in the wake of the kamikaze experience. The quad 40mm mounts amidships and their directors are the centre of attention. The sponsons for the Bofors were moved forward of the aft stack, partly for stability reasons but also to improve the arc of fire of the quads. (USN)

The *Brownson* was the first of the new 117 square-bridge configurations, the rest following fairly quickly as wartime mass production kicked into gear. The speed of construction and demand for destroyers precluded much variation.

In general terms, as they came in for refit during 1943-44 the AA armament of the round-bridge destroyers was upgraded to that of the square-bridge ships, but with more varied results. Some kept the aft 40mm; some of the others did not install 40mm on the forward deckhouse, retaining the 20mm instead. By the end of 1944 almost all of the *Fletchers*, square- and round-bridge, had eight or more 40mm AA and were of roughly the same configuration. This was not enough, however, to cope with the latest threat – the kamikaze. This one weapon was to cause more damage to *Fletcher* class destroyers than any other single source.

Left: Another dockyard photo of the *Howorth* taken on the same day showing the ship from forward. (USN)

Miller (DD 535) on 24 August 1945 showing off the full range of the anti-kamikaze measures, including the enhanced electronics suite. (USN)

In April 1945, as a result of the kamikaze attacks, a program to strengthen the anti-aircraft at the expense of torpedo armament was implemented. There was not much left to torpedo anyway, so the sacrifice was not crucial. Fifty-three *Fletcher* class destroyers were modified to a new standard. The 40mm twins abreast the aft stack were eliminated and the supporting sponsons were enlarged and moved forward 10ft. In these larger gun tubs 40mm quads were located, bringing the total number of 40mm barrels to fourteen. The single 20mm mounts were replaced by 20mm twins, making the total 20mm armament fourteen barrels. The torpedo tubes between the stacks were removed and a platform for the Mk 51 40mm gun directors was installed. The platform on the aft stack (where the Mk 51s were earlier) was removed to reduce top-weight. A small mast was added just forward of the aft 40mm gun tub. This mast supported two radomes.

The upgrade program started in April 1945 but only seven or eight of the new-look *Fletchers* made it to the combat zone. The *Yarnell*, *Clarence Bronson*, *Cotton*, *Dortch*, *Gatling*, *Healy* and *Halsey Powell* were all modified in time to be among the destroyers attending the surrender ceremony in Tokyo Bay. However since the four 'museum' *Fletchers* and most of the post-war *Fletchers* were configured this way, it has become the look of a 'typical' *Fletcher*.

After the war many of the *Fletchers* were laid up. A portion of those that remained on active duty were further modernised, generally increasing their electronics, ASW and AAW capability. Most sprouted tripod masts forward to support the additional radar and other electronic equipment. Some of them lost their No 2 gunhouse – replaced by a Hedgehog or Weapon Alfa. The 40mm quads were replaced by 3in/50 twins. In some the aft 40mm twin was replaced by a 3in/50 twin. They all lost their depth charge throwers. Even with all the modifications they retained their distinctive silhouette and were unmistakeably *Fletchers*.

The *Jenkins* (DD 447), on 14 August 1942 just after commissioning, in a splotch pattern. Note the lighter colours above the deck line. This is especially visible on the stacks. (USN)

CAMOUFLAGE

Camouflage schemes make the most dramatic difference in the appearance of ships. In the US Navy they are described by the camouflage Measure and Pattern. The camouflage Measure describes the colours to be used. If there is a second set of numbers (/16, /24, etc), it describes the Pattern – the areas of the ship where the colours go (and of course the design). The letter following the design number describes the type of vessel for which the design was originally prepared: D for Destroyer, B for Battleship, C for cruiser, etc, but this does not mean that a C design was limited to cruisers only. A glance at the table below shows that nine *Fletcher* class destroyers were painted in a cruiser design in 1944. An example of how this works would be Ms 32 /6D, where Ms 32 specifies that the colours Haze Gray, Ocean Gray and Navy Blue, 6D describes the pattern, where D stands for destroyer type.

The original seven *Fletchers* were commissioned in a camouflage pattern called Measure 13 Modified. This was known as a splotch camouflage and the underlying colour was Haze Gray. On the hull there were irregular patterns of Ocean Gray or even Navy Blue. Above the hull there were lighter splotches of Light Gray. It was a very loosely specified pattern – basically the guidelines were very informal and the ships looked however their captain wanted them to look.

However, these ships were all painted in Ms 21 (which is all vertical surfaces Navy Blue and all horizontal surfaces Deck Blue) prior to sailing for the Solomon Islands and combat. With very few exceptions the *Fletchers* were in Ms 21 camouflage in the Solomon Islands and other combat zones from

The *Jenkins* in the combat zone in 1943, appearing in a very worn looking Measure 21 camouflage of Navy Blue throughout. (USN)

Pattern	Measure 31	Measure 32
1D	533	468, 528, 529, 583, 584, 586
2D		476
3D	585	446, 590, 673, 679
6D	564, 798	447, 521, 550, 563, 591, 654, 655, 801
7D	552, 792	466, 477, 682, 793
9D	465, 656, 669, 681, 687	
10D	544, 660, 661,	519, 644
11D	567, 593, 642, 799, 802, 804	474, 595, 667
13D		475, 478, 515, 560, 562, 577, 651, 653, 662, 664, 678, 685, 686, 690, 794, 795, 800
14D		516, 569, 570, 575, 578, 579, 675, 676
16D	481, 520, 556, 571, 572, 594, 630, 658, 674, 797, 803	561, 565, 566, 580
18D		511, 522, 663
21D	500, 507, 508, 672	471, 540, 545, 553, 559, 588, 649, 683
22D	592, 684	
23D	534, 568, 665	
24D	448, 449, 527	531, 532
2C	445, 509, 512, 514, 541, 573, 657, 796	
14C	513	

October 1942 until early 1944.

In 1944 a new type of camouflage was adopted, known as 'splinter' or 'dazzle' camouflage or more formally Measures 31, 32 or 33. It looked like a crazy quilt but it had a more serious purpose. The idea behind these types of camouflage was not to reduce the visibility of the ship, but the strange patterns were designed to confuse the enemy as to the identity, course and bearing of the ship for targeting purposes. From a modelling perspective these dazzle camouflages look very striking and are popular subjects.

Above is a table of which DDs were painted in which Measure and Pattern. Measure 31 was a dark pattern using Dull Black, Navy Blue, Ocean Gray and Haze Gray as colours. Measure 32 was a medium pattern, which used Dull Black (and to a lesser extent) Navy Blue, Ocean Gray, Haze Gray And Light Gray. The decks were also painted in a pattern of Deck Blue and Ocean Gray.

In late 1944 the kamikaze menace forced a rethink of camouflage. Splinter camouflage may have confused the enemy as to identity and course but it made the ship itself highly visible. A kamikaze pilot had little interest in a target's course and identity – he wanted to crash into anything that he could see. So in early 1945 there was a massive repainting of the Pacific Fleet into Measures 21 and 22. Initially ships were painted in Measure 21 as it made them less visible to aircraft, but as the kamikaze threat receded Measure 22 came into favour. Most of the *Fletchers*

The *Van Valkenberg* (DD 656) on 7 August 1944 sporting a striking looking dazzle camouflage. This one conforms to Measure 31/9D. (USN)

Left: *Benham* (DD 796) in January 1944 wearing pattern 2C of Measure 31, one of the designs nominally intended for cruisers. (USN)

Below: Another variant of Measure 31 carried here by *Bullard* (DD 660) in November 1944 is 10D. (USN)

ended the war painted in Measure 22.

The advent of radar made visibility a less important issue, and after the war the ships reverted to Measure 13 – Haze Gray overall. However, the specification for Measure 13 had changed slightly. The decks were now painted Dark Gray rather than Deck Blue. And so they remained until the end of their service life in the US Navy.

Years and camouflage types:
1942 – Ms 13, 21, 22
1944 – Ms 31, Ms 32
1945 – Ms 21, 22
1946 – Haze Gray (Ms 13 revived)

Below: The *Hart* (DD 594) on 19 February 1944, freshly painted in Ms 22 camouflage. (USN)

Fletcher 1942

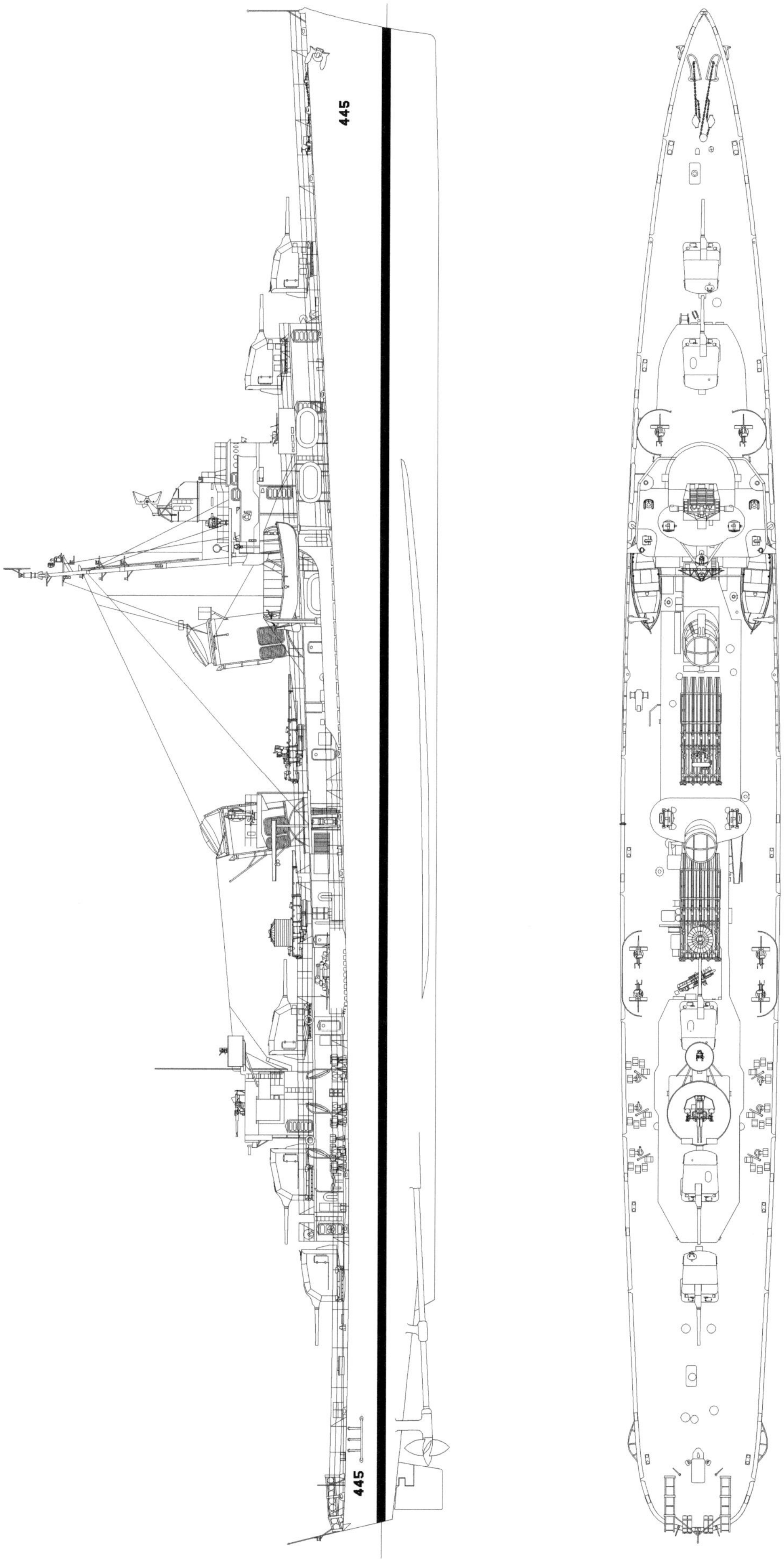

Stevens 1943

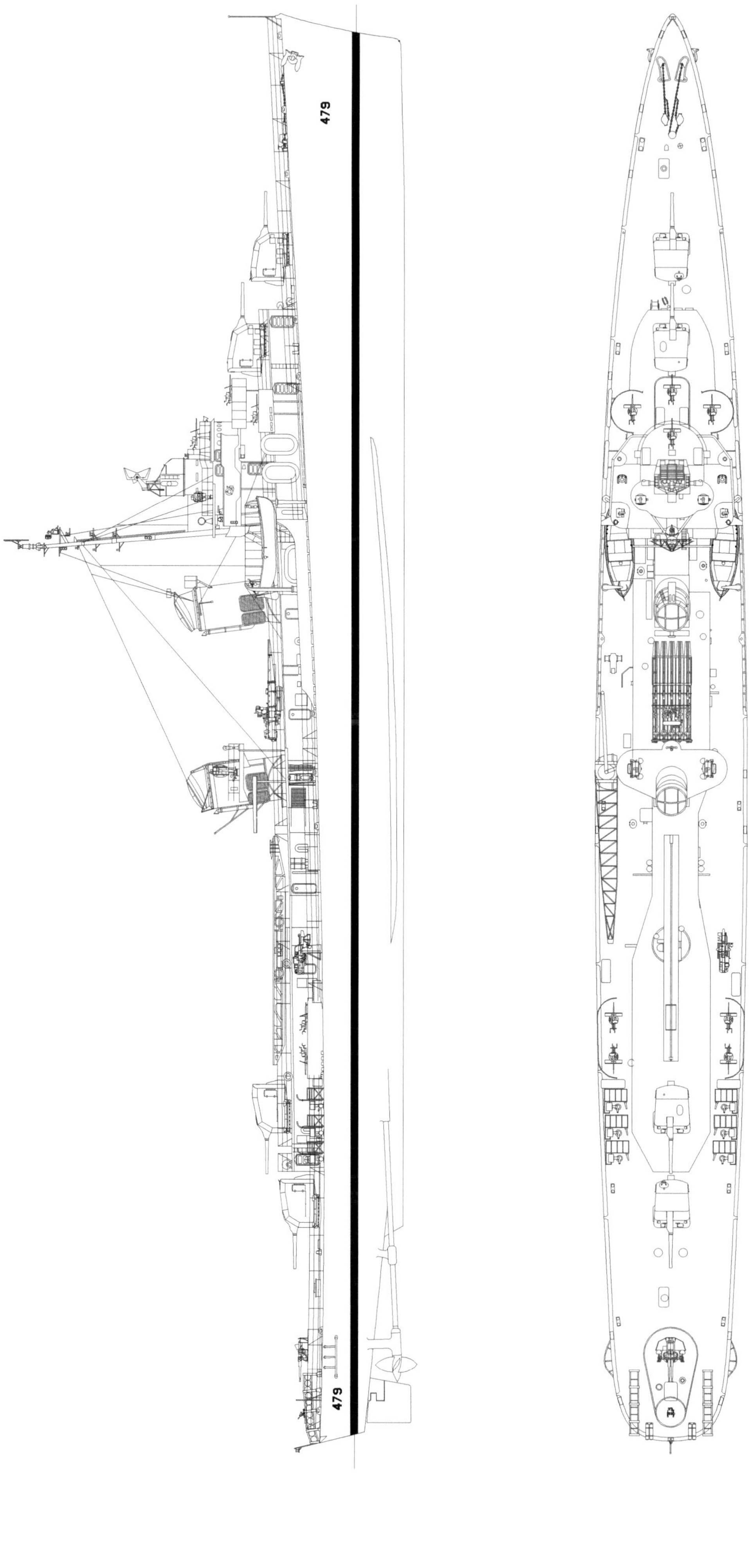

Hoel 1944

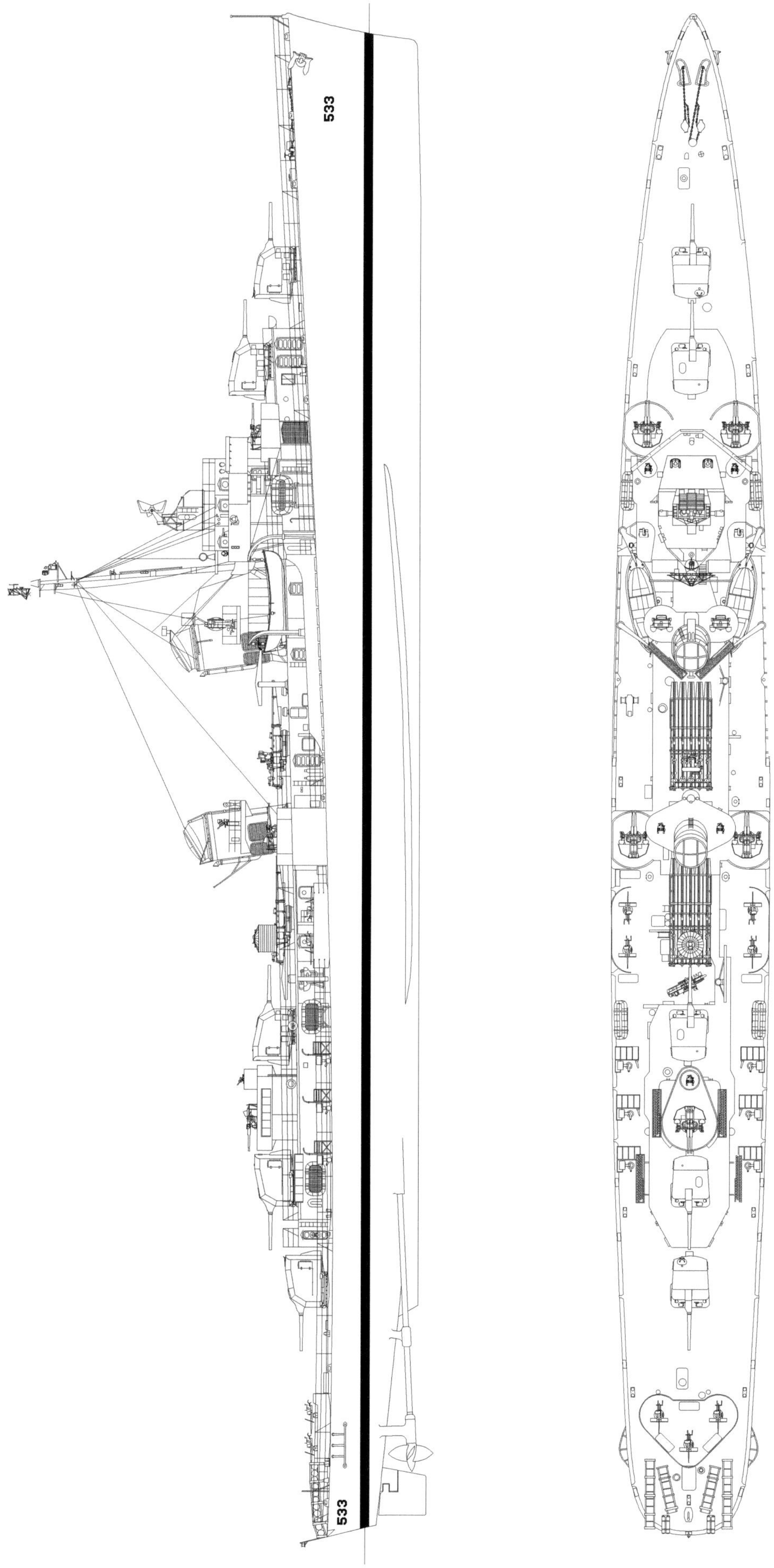

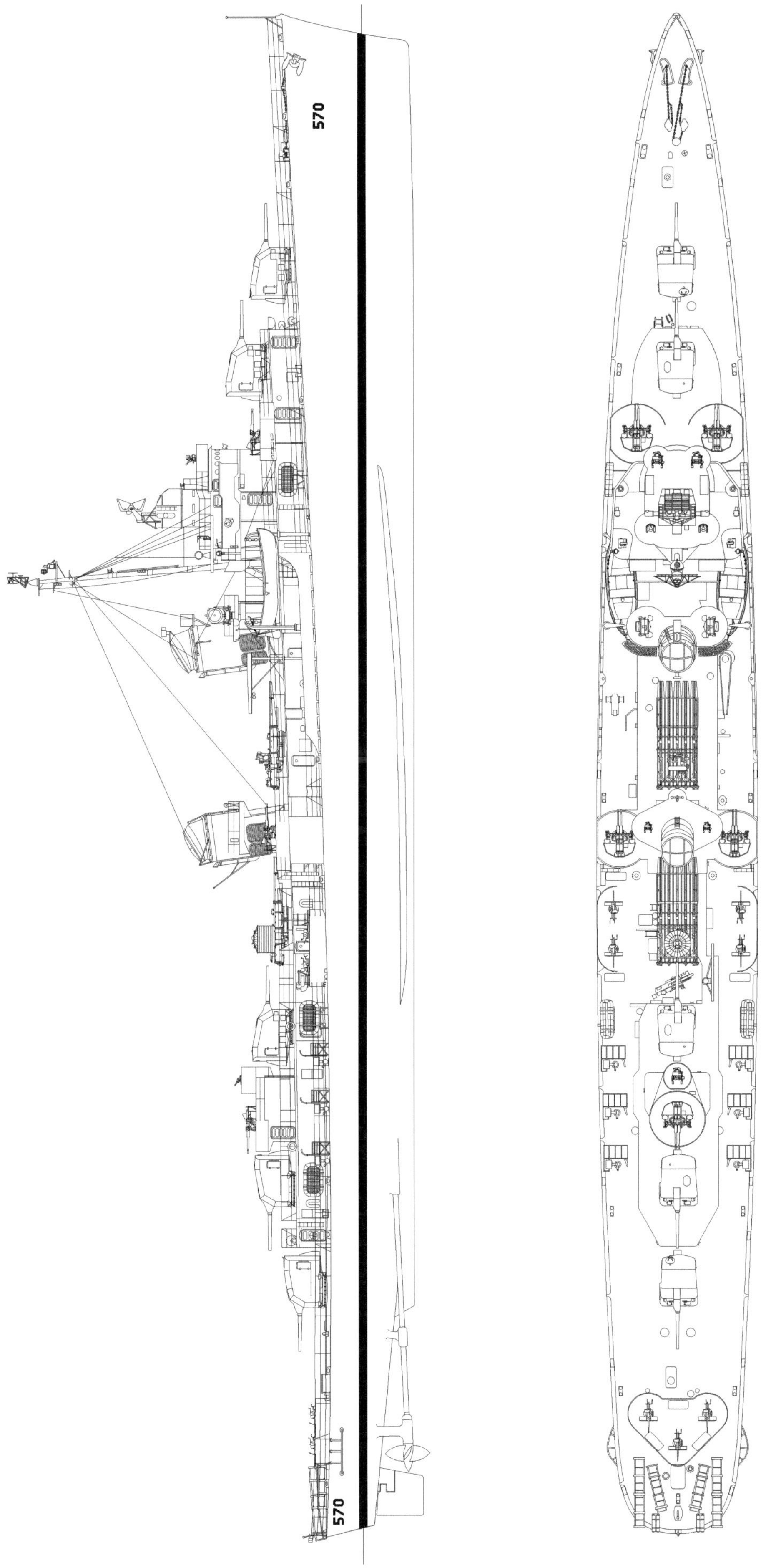

Charles Ausburne 1944

Stoddard 1944

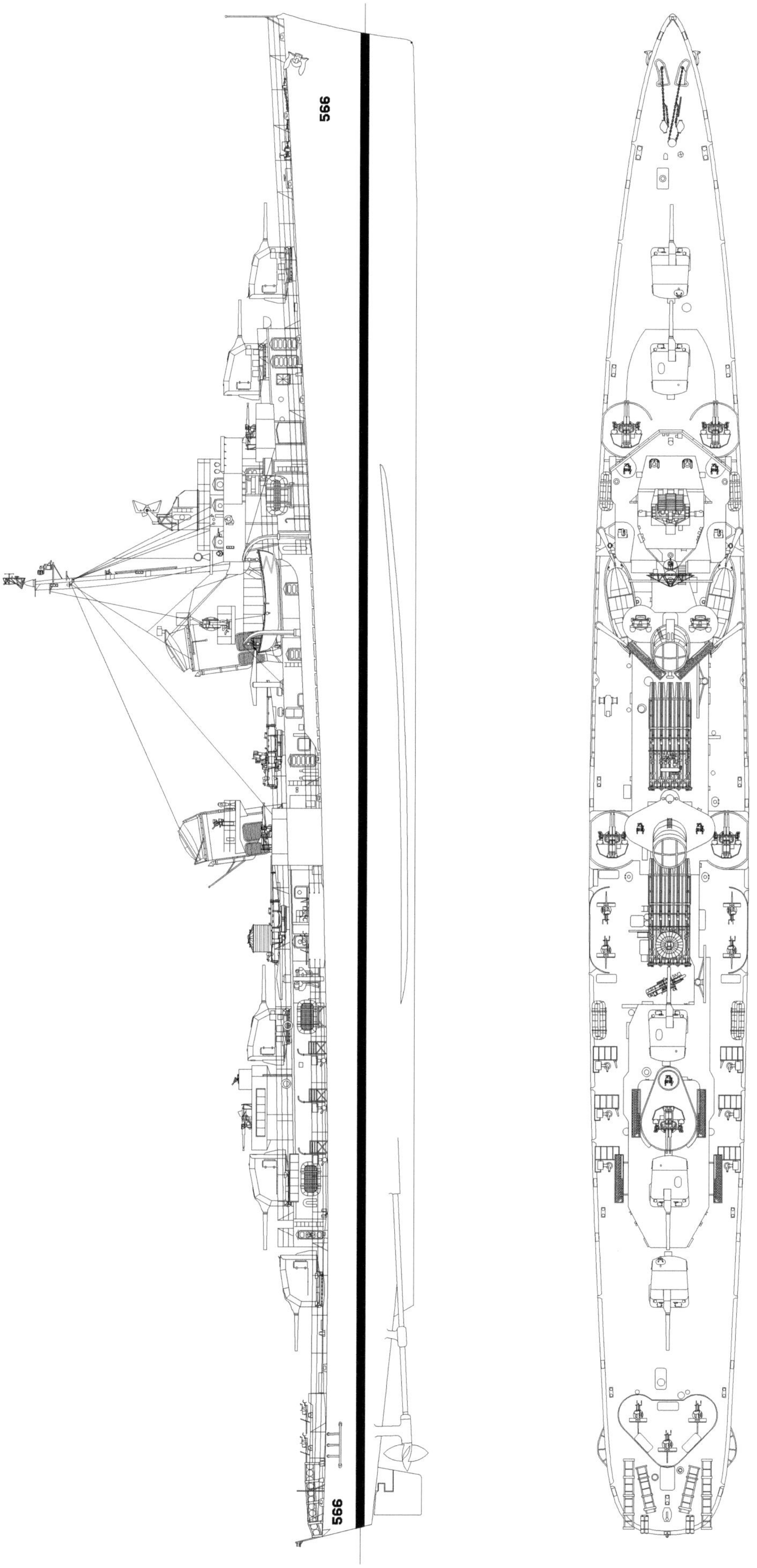

Heermann 1944

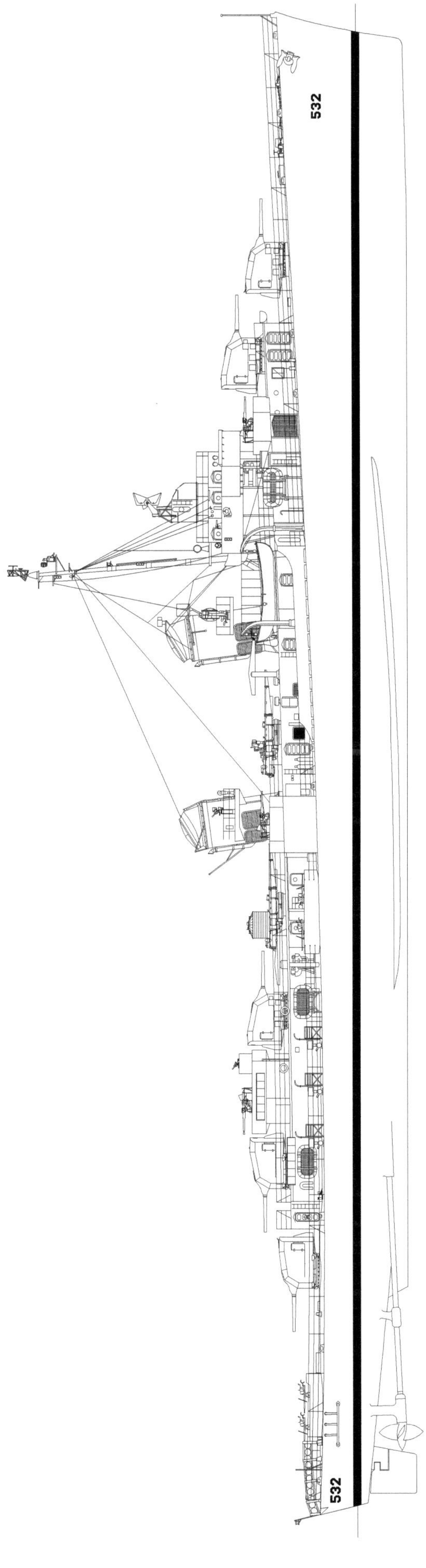

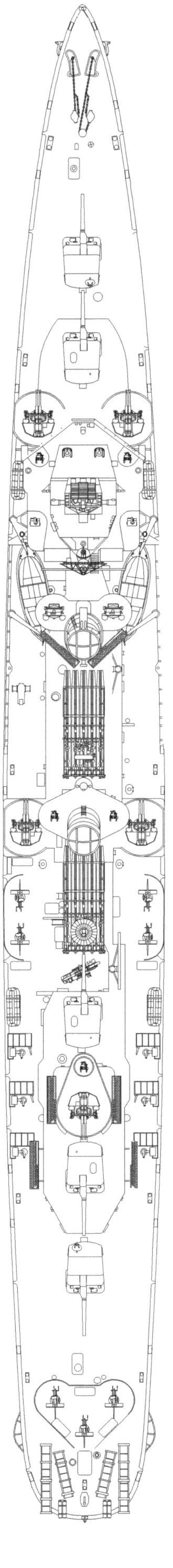

***Kidd* 1945**

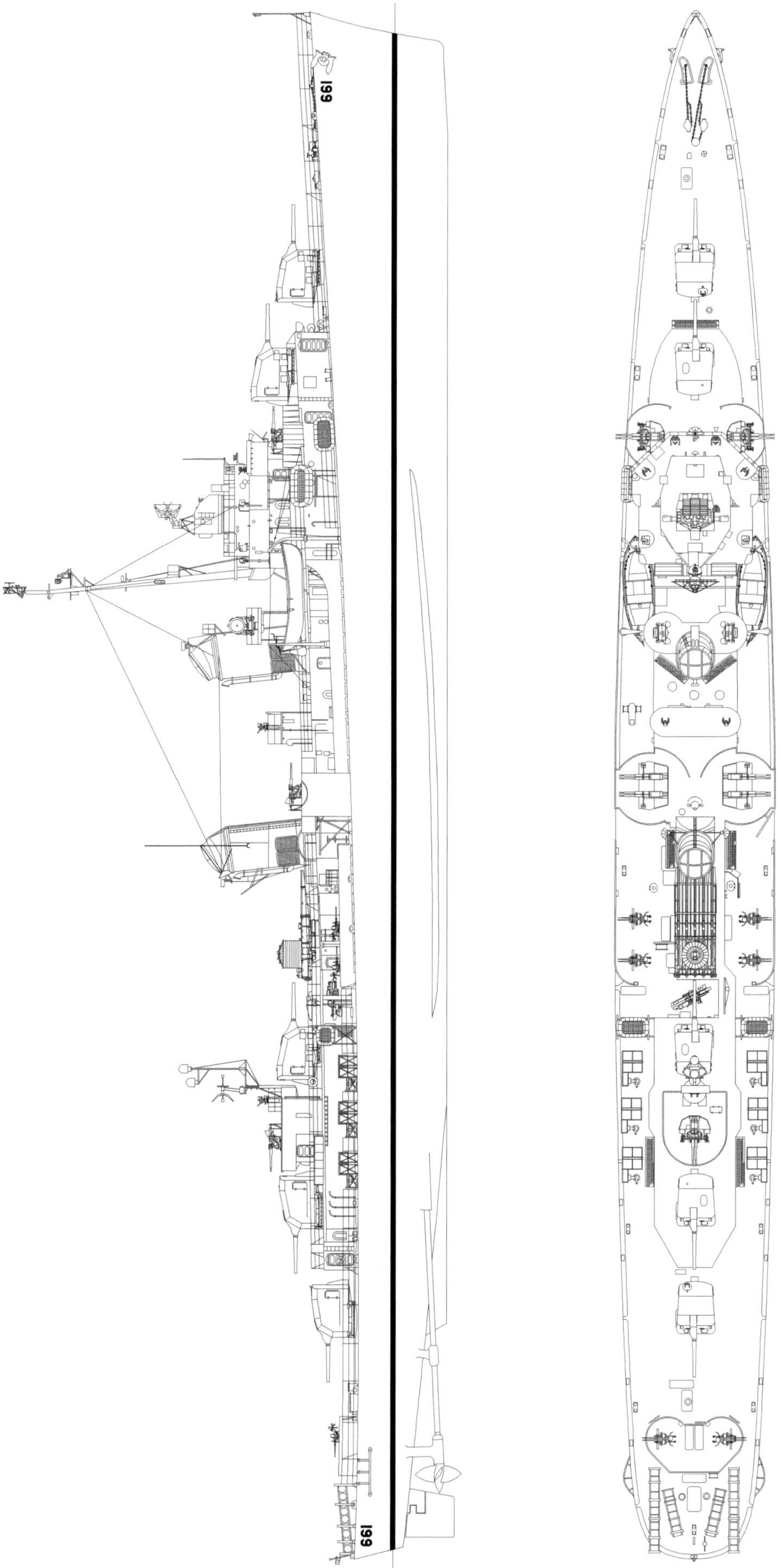

SELECTED REFERENCES

Roscoe, Theodore, *United States Destroyer Operations in World War II,* Naval Institute Press, Annapolis, MD 1953.

Friedman, Norman, *Destroyer Design History,* Naval Institute Press, Annapolis, MD 1982.

Scutts, Jerry, *Fletcher Class Destroyers*, Squadron/Signal Publications, Carrollton, TX 1995.

Cutler, Thomas J, *The Battle of Leyte Gulf*, Harper Collins, New York 1994.

Grace, James W, *The Naval Battle of Guadalcanal, Night Action 13 November 1942*, Naval Institute Press, Annapolis, MD 1999.

Sumrall, Robert & Walkowiak, Thomas, *USS Kidd*, Pictorial Histories Publishing Company, Missoula, MT 1985.

Harmon, J Scott, *USS Cassin Young, A Fletcher Class Destroyer*, Pictorial Histories Publishing Company, Missoula, MT 1984.

Preston, Anthony, *Destroyers,* Bison Books, London 1982.

Walkowiak, Thomas & Sowinski, Larry, *United States Navy Camouflage of the WW 2 Era Part 1*, The Floating Drydock, Philadelphia, PA 1976, 1988.

Morison, Samuel Eliot, *History of US Naval Operations in WWII*, Vols: *V The Struggle for Guadalcanal*; *VI Breaking the Bismarcks Barrier*; *VII Aleutians, Gilberts and Marshalls*; *VIII New Guinea and the Marianas*; *XII Leyte*; *XIII Liberation of the Philippines*; *XIV Victory in the Pacific*; *XV Supplement and General Index*, Little Brown and Co, Boston 1951, 1960.

Robert Stern, *US Navy 1942 – 1943,* Arms and Armour Press, London 1990.

WARSHIP MODELLING WEBSITES

www.deansmarine.co.uk
www.dynamicdioramas.com
www.ipmsusa.com
www.jdproduct.com
www.modelwarships.com
www.smmlonline.com
www.steelnavy.com
www.scaleshipyard.com
www.warshipmodelsunderway.com

WARSHIP RESEARCH WEBSITES

www.classicwarships.com
www.destroyerhistory.org/fletcherclass/
www.hazegray.org
www.historycentral.com/NAVY/destroyer.
www.history.navy.mil
www.shipcamouflage.com/warship_camouflage.htm
www.navsource.org

AUTHOR'S ACKNOWLEDGEMENTS

Steve Wiper, David Empson, Nan Lin, Loren Perry, Joseph Neumeyer, Don Pruel, Kurt Greiner, Cathy Owen, Elizabeth Abbey

At the end of the war the *Fletcher* class reverted to the overall Haze Gray of a revived Measure 13. This is *Howorth* (DD 592) on 10 January 1946.